POWER PACK ENGLISH

Skills and strategies for advanced learners

by Klaus Hinz, Herbert Holtwisch
and Karl Heinz Wagner

Editor: Klaus Hinz

Linguistic adviser: Harold Fish

Best.-Nr. 040480 8

Schöningh

www.schoeningh.de
Schöningh Verlag, Jühenplatz 1–3, 33098 Paderborn

Druck A 5 4 3 / Jahr 2007 06 05
Alle Drucke der Serie A sind im Unterricht parallel verwendbar.
Die letzte Zahl bezeichnet das Jahr dieses Druckes.

Umschlaggestaltung: INNOVA, Borchen
Druck und Bindung: westermann druck GmbH, Braunschweig

ISBN 3-14-040480-8

Contents

Preface

To the student

Power Pack English will help you to become an independent and successful learner.
The aim of the book is to help you read, understand and analyse English texts that are used in class and examinations and to teach you how to write English texts of your own.
The explanation of a technique is followed by an example and a task so that you get the chance to test yourself. You will find the solution in the booklet *Solutions*.

The book contains basic learning strategies, reading and writing techniques including examples how to write exam papers and also shows how to analyse visual and listening texts as well as films. The book ends up with a register related to technical and literary terms you come across in the book. You also find lists of words and phrases that you will need for talking about and writing English texts.

You can either study the whole book, work on one chapter only when you feel that some gaps need to be filled or you can use it as a reference book whenever you feel unsafe about a particular point.

To the teacher

Power Pack English systematically teaches the skills and strategies that students need to solve any task in an advanced English class. It provides carefully selected material for text reception and text production and gives learners as much practical help as possible. The term text is used in its widest sense and comprises literary and non-literary texts, listening texts such as interviews or radio plays and audio-visual media texts such as films or video films.

The main intention of the book has been to increase the students' competence in understanding and writing English texts. They learn precisely how to approach texts, how to analyse and evaluate them and even how to produce longer texts of their own. In a word, *Power Pack English* promotes the competence in the fields of text comprehension, text analysis, text appreciation, and text production.

The approach incorporates the latest thinking in methodology and psychology of learning and describes in detail how to tackle a task as a process: 1) What has to be done before beginning a task, 2) what while doing it and 3) what after having finished it?

Power Pack English is a methodological handbook which can be used along with any reader in English courses. When a special technique, e.g. reading, has to be introduced or improved the respective chapter of the book can be dealt with. Should you only need to improve one text form, e.g. writing a creative text, you will only have to work on the relevant sequence. The approach is as comprehensive as possible so that – after studying the material – the students will feel prepared for any task in their English class.

Basic learning strategies

Strategies mean doing something systematically and methodically, they help you to learn and to become independent. As an advanced student you need a variety of basic skills, e.g. organising materials and your work place, managing time, developing your own learning strategies and using different sources of information.

Organising materials and your work place

Study materials

- Organise your classroom materials such as handouts, notes, assignments, etc. A ring binder can help you get organised because different kinds of materials can be stored in it.

Home study area

- You need to keep your study area (desk, table, etc.) organised so that books, dictionary, grammar book, paper, pencils and other supplies are always close at hand.
  Even if you haven't got a room of your own you need a fixed place for study. Use the best possible environment. It should be quiet and relatively free of distractions like radio, TV, etc.

Managing your time

Organising a time table

Monitoring time

- One of the best techniques for using time efficiently is to prepare a time schedule, a programme of work to be done.
  Write down things you have to do in a weekly and in a long term planner and tick off tasks you have been able to do.

  Weekly planner (tasks you have to do shortly):

	Short term task	long term task	extra work	✓
Monday Tuesday ...				

Long term planner (tasks you will have to do within the next weeks):

	long term task	extra work (reviewing vocabulary/grammar/reading and writing techniques)
Week 1		
Week 2		
Week 3		
...		

- Find out when your most productive study periods are. The time between 8 and 12 in the morning and between 4 and 6 in the afternoon is usually most efficient. Try to study at the same time every day and don't work on a full stomach, i.e. shortly after a meal.

Pauses

- Pauses are very important.
  Mind this formula: Working time = studying + pauses.
  Every 30 minutes a 5 minute pause!

Setting reasonable goals

Study goals

- Divide your task into sections. Set small short-range goals for yourself and set a time when you will have finished each task.

Concentration

- Concentration is very important during your study period. If your mind wanders, stand up and face away from your books. Don't sit at your desk staring into the book or daydreaming.

Developing your own learning strategies

Self-responsibility

- Take responsibility for your own learning, for instance when your knowledge of English grammar has many gaps or when you need some more writing practice. Organise your learning process on your own and start learning independently.

Self-evaluation

- You need to learn to evaluate your strengths and weaknesses. In principle there are two ways to do this:
  a) Listing the mistakes you have made in written exams,
  b) filling in a self-evaluation sheet that you can make up yourself.
  Both methods show your weaknesses that should be cured.

a) List of mistakes made in written exams

mistakes	Test 1	Test 2	Test 3	Test 4
Vocabulary words idioms phrases spelling				
Grammar tenses gerunds/participles reported speech if-clauses relative clauses etc.				

Vocabulary: The table indicates which word field(s) you should work on. To increase your word power collect words, note them down in a topic diagram (a table containing word columns), put it in your binder and learn the words. Use the time planner for your revision work.

Pollution

air pollution	phrases	water pollution
emission of pollutants into the atmosphere smog smoke harmful gas chemical poisons fumes from motor vehicles …	polluted with … contaminated with … to cause pollution to avoid pollution free from pollution to pump water into … to produce thick smoke …	oil sewage industrial waste detergent[1] fertiliser effluent[2] …

Difficult words can be explained in footnotes, e.g.: [1] *Waschmittel* – [2] liquid waste matter, e.g. from a factory

Grammar: The table also shows which grammatical problems you need to practise. Look them up in your grammar book, note down patterns and grammar rules in your note-book and do some exercises. Plan some time in your weekly and long term planner.

b) Self-evaluation sheet

Example: "Reading a short story"

Personal rection

Have I enjoyed reading the short story?

☐ Yes, quite a lot. ☐ No, not much because ____________________

☐ Yes, a little. ☐ Not at all because ____________________

Difficulties

Was it difficult to understand the story?

☐ No, because ____________________

☐ Yes, very difficult because ____________________

☐ Some passages were difficult because ____________________

Using a dictionary

Did I have to use a dictionary?

☐ Yes, very often, in order to understand the text.

☐ Only sometimes, in order to ____________________

☐ No.

Using different reading techniques

How did I read the text?

☐ I read the whole story from beginning to end very slowly and intensively.

☐ I read the introduction and the parts containing lots of information very slowly, other parts faster (extensively).

☐ I need to improve my reading skills in order to be able to read longer texts.

☐ I think I should enlarge my vocabulary in order to be able to read texts without difficulty.

The analysis may show that you are fond of reading, but that your reading speed is rather slow and that you have to practise reading techniques. (→ How to read – reading skills, pp. 11–16)

Using different sources of information

There are various sources (books and modern information technology) to help you overcome problems when you write a text or do some project work.

- **Dictionaries**
  When you come across linguistic problems a dictionary is a great help with vocabulary problems (→ Context and dictionary: How to guess the meaning of words, pp. 15–16). You may use the "Dictionary of Contemporary English" (Longman), the "Oxford Advanced Learner's Dictionary" (Cornelsen & Oxford) or the "Essential Activator" (Longman).

Linguistic questions

- **Grammar books**
  If you are not sure about a grammatical problem look it up in your grammar book and study the respective paragraphs.
- **Readers**
  Readers for advanced students contain chapters on different topics. Look up the table of contents and skim over or scan the texts about the topic for which you need some information. (→ Skimming, scanning, p. 12)

Content questions

- **Reference books**
  There are various reference books you can use, e.g. the Encyclopaedia Britannica, which is also available on CD-ROM. You find the information you want by typing a word, phrase, or question in the keyword field, for instance "Constitution: USA". The search engine returns a list of article titles, ordered by relevance, e.g.:

  Entries for: Constitution: USA
  715 found in the Encyclopaedia Britannica (1–10)
  - Constitution of the United States of America
  - Constitutional law: Judicial review in the United States
  - Atlantic Constitution
  - Constitution: Constitutionality
  - Year in Review 1995: media-and-publishing: Newspaper world affairs: Special Report
  - Madison, James: father of the Constitution
  - civil constitution of the Clergy
  - Constitution
  - Spain, history of: The Constitution of Cadiz

  Click "Constitution of the United States" and you will get a text on the history of the Constitution. If you click "Constitution of the United States" again (in the text), you will have the complete wording of the Constitution.
- **Internet**
  The Internet is the latest in modern information and communication technology. You can get information by directly accessing homepages such as www.layouth.com for *Los Angeles Youth* or www.mirror.co.uk for *The Mirror* or by using search engines, such as www.altavista.com, www.lycos.com, www.yahoo.com, www.google.com, etc.

Example: Search engine "google"

Enter www.google.com on the starting page, type "Constitution USA" for the search and click here to start the search.

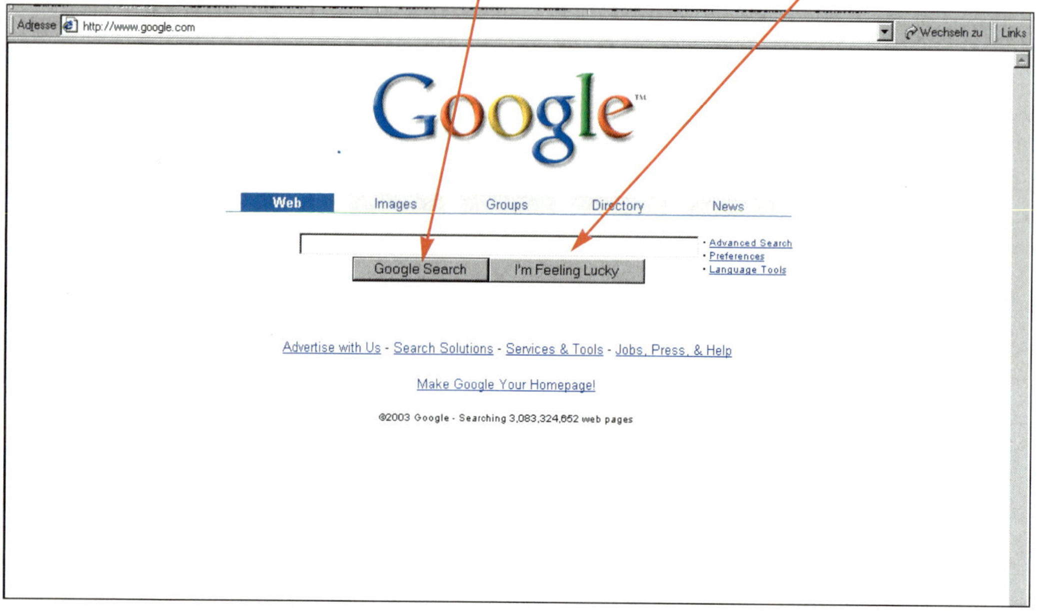

You will get several web sites to choose from.
Click here to get the text.

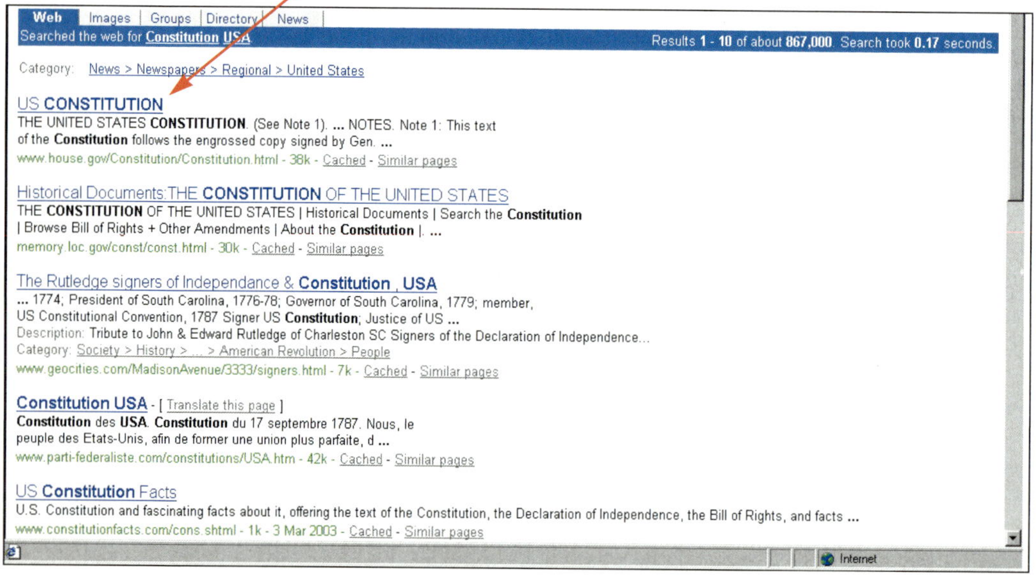

How to read – reading skills

The P – R – R reading method

The **P-R-R reading method** helps you to make the most out of your reading. It consists of three steps: **P** = Preview![1], **R** = Read actively! and **R** = Review![2].

Before reading (P)

Preview!

When you have a general idea of the contents of a text, you will be better able to understand what you will read later.

- Anticipate[3] the contents of the text!
  Look at the title, subheadings, pictures, words in bold type[4], the first sentence(s), etc. and guess what the text may be about.
- Reactivate your pre-knowledge[5]!
  Ask yourself, what you already know about the topic/theme. What would you like to learn from the text?

While reading (R)

Read actively!

You should always use "pen in hand" to make your reading effective.

- Underline or mark important points you have just read.
- Take notes from the text and jot them down in the margin or on a sheet of paper.

After reading (R)

Review!

Re-reading is helpful for full comprehension.

- Review your notes and read the points/information belonging to them again.
- Summarise the main points or enter them in a chart.
- Think about what you would like to discuss in class.

[1] **to preview** to look ahead – [2] **to review** to examine, to check – [3] **to anticipate** to expect sth. – [4] **in bold type** *in Fettdruck* – [5] **pre-knowledge** what you already know

Reading purposes and reading strategies

We distinguish three different kinds of reading purposes and corresponding reading strategies: **reading for gist** (extensive reading), **reading for special points** (selective reading), and **reading for detail** (intensive reading).

Reading for gist: extensive reading

- When you only want to get a general impression or the main points of a text, you **skim** through or over it, i.e. you read the text quickly and ignore irrelevant sentences or passages.
- Put down what you have found in one or two sentences.

Reading for special points: selective reading

- When you want to find information about special points, you **scan** the text, i.e. you read quickly and pause whenever you come across the information you are looking for.
- Mark the text or write notes in the margin.

Reading for detail: intensive reading

- When you want to understand as many details as possible you will have to read the text slowly and will sometimes have to use a dictionary.
- Underline the most important information in the text, fill in a note-taking chart or summarise your findings.

Example

The following text demonstrates three reading approaches. So you have to read the text three times.

Tasks:

1. What is the following text about? (Reading for gist)
2. How has fox-hunting developed? (Reading for special points)
3. Describe fox-hunting and a fox-hunting day. (Reading for detail)

Fox-hunting

blue marking = special points

In England, the home of the sport, fox-hunting dates from at least the 15th century. Opinion varies as to when it originated. In its inception[1], it was probably an adjunct[2] to stag and hare hunting, with the same hounds used to chase each quarry[3].

description of ↓ fox-hunting (yellow marking)

Modern fox-hunting took shape in the 19th century shortly after Hugo Meynell – the father of the modern English chase – started hunting; and it soon developed into a national upper-class pastime. Traditional procedure is still observed and the proper kit[4] worn. A fox hunt is conducted by the master, and, in theory, all who take part in it do so at his invitation even when they pay for the privilege. The hounds, generally 15 to 20 couples (matched pairs), are controlled by the huntsman, who may be the master himself but who is generally the senior paid servant of the hunt. Two or three whippers-in[5] assist in reconnaissance[6] and in keeping the hounds together as a pack. Master, huntsman, and whippers-in take precedence[7] over all other riders to hounds. The huntsman controls hounds by voice, his calls being known as cheers, and by his horn – a copper tube about eight inches long – that produces two notes of great carrying and penetrating quality.

A day's hunting begins with a meet, at which the followers join the hounds, acknowledge the master, and are frequently offered hospitality by one of their number who acts as host for the occasion. On the command of the master, hounds move off to draw (search) the covert[8], which may be woodland, a patch of gorse, or a field in which it is suspected that a fox may be. When the fox is found, the fact being signalled by the cry of hounds, notes of the horn, and the shout "Tallyho," the hunt begins and ordinarily proceeds to the stage at which the fox is viewed, a moment signalled by a holloa, a high-pitched cry. If a kill follows, the brush (tail), mask (head), and pads (feet) of the fox may be given as trophies by the master to any followers whom he considers to deserve the honour. The body of the fox is then thrown to the hounds. […]

↓ a hunting day

Before World War I, fox-hunting reached a zenith of popularity as an English field sport. Horse und hound had arrived at a highly developed state, and hunting itself was well organised and regulated by the Master of Foxhounds Association.

[1] **inception** starting point – [2] **adjunct** a thing added to sth. – [3] **quarry** animal pursued by a hunter – [4] **kit** clothing and equipment of a huntsman – [5] **whipper-in** person responsible for controlling the hounds during a hunt – [6] **reconnaissance** exploration or survey of an area – [7] **precedence** right to come before sb. in order or rank – [8] **covert** a thicket in which the fox can hide

Solution

1. What is the text about?
   The text deals with the development of chasing a fox by horsemen with a pack of hounds.

   Reading for gist: extensive reading

2. How has fox-hunting developed?
   Fox-hunting
   dates from at least the 15th century,
   took shape in the 19th century, and
   reached the zenith of popularity in the 20th century.

   Reading for special points: selective reading

Reading for detail: intensive reading

3. Describe fox-hunting and a fox-hunting day.

fox hunting	hunting day
• practised since the 15th century • upper-class pastime • conducted by the master • 15 to 20 couples of hounds controlled by the huntsman • two/three whippers-in assist in keeping the hounds together as a pack • master, huntsman and whippers-in ranking higher than other riders	• begins with a meeting • on the command of the master hounds start searching the area • when a fox is found the hunt begins • tail, head and feet of a killed fox are given as trophies to any followers • body of the fox is thrown to the hounds

Reading speed

Reading rapidly is a useful skill in school and in real life. Comprehension is even better at higher rates of speed. In order to read rapidly and well you need to have the necessary vocabulary and comprehension skills but also have to know certain reading techniques.

Reading techniques: What to do and what to avoid

Avoid moving lips

- Don't pronounce or whisper words as you read because then your reading speed will be slower.

Read by word groups

- Don't read word by word, but rather look at groups of words (phrases or sense units).

  Don't read word by word:

  Eliminate[1] the habit of pronouncing words as you read. If you sound out words in your throat or whisper them, you can read only as fast as you can read aloud.

  but in word groups like this:

  Eliminate the habit of pronouncing words as you read.
  If you sound out words in your throat or whisper them,
  you can read only as fast as you can read aloud.

[1] **to eliminate** to completely get rid of sth.

Adjust[1] reading speed to reading purpose

- Determine the reading purpose before reading.
  If you only need main ideas, skim over the text (→ Skimming, p. 12) – don't feel you must read every word.
  But if you read analytically, read at a slow speed to allow other ideas (→ examples, p. 14).

Adjust reading speed to the nature of text material

- Adjust your reading speed to the difficulty of the text you are reading. The more difficult it is the slower your reading speed will normally be.

Context and dictionary: How to guess the meaning of words

There are mainly two ways to learn the meaning of unknown words: guessing the meaning from **context** and using a **dictionary**.
The so-called analytical method, i.e. finding the meaning of a word with the help of word formation (e.g. apply – applicable – applicant – application), similarities between English and German or other languages (e.g. characterise – charakterisieren) etc. can be used with some words but it is very limited.

Using the context

The context, i.e. the words and sentences that come before or after the unknown word, helps you to guess the meaning of a word. The more information a sentence contains the easier it will be for you to guess the meaning of unknown words.

- Read the sentence and pay attention to the context, to the information it contains.
- Ask yourself what the word could mean in that specific context.
- It is sufficient to find a rough idea of the word.

Examples:

We sat at the table by the window, watching the rain slap against the glass.
(How, do you think, rain can hit the window pane? – Solution: slap = *klatschen*)

The boys decided to go out for a walk and changed into their outdoor gear.
(What do people normally change into before walking out? – Solution: outdoor gear = *Straßenkleidung*)

[1] **to adjust** *anpassen*

Using a dictionary

Looking up a word in a dictionary means interrupting your reading again and again. You should only do so if you urgently need to know the exact meaning of a word.

- Check which word class (noun, verb, adjective, etc.) the word you are looking for belongs to.
- Look the word up in an English-English dictionary. The word class is given after the headword.
- Different meanings for a particular word are indicated by numbers. Read all the definitions and the examples as well, they will help you to find the right meaning.

pronunciation — British English — American English — definition

headword → **coach**[1] /kəʊtʃ/ *n* **1** *BrE* || **bus** *AmE*- a comfortable bus used for long-distance travel or touring: *We went to Switzerland by coach.* | *This hotel welcomes coach parties* (= groups of people travelling in coaches) **2** also **carriage** *BrE* || **car** *AmE* – a railway passenger carriage **3** a person **a** who trains sportsmen and sportswomen for games, competitions, etc.: *a football/baseball coach* **b** who is employed privately to train a student for an examination: *a mathematics coach* **4** a large enclosed four-wheeled horse-drawn carriage, used esp. in former times or in official ceremonies: *a coach and four* (= four horses) | *the royal coach* – see picture at CARRIAGE

(1st, 2nd, 3rd and 4th meaning)

coach[2] *v* [I;T (for, in)] to train or teach, esp. not in a place of formal education: give instruction or advice to (a person or a group of people): *I coach people for English exams.* | *She coaches me in French.* | *to do some private coaching* – see TEACH (USAGE)

(word class) (← example)

Examples:

David: "I'll be sitting in the second **coach** from the front of the train." Coach: noun; the second meaning is the right one. (Solution: [a railway-passenger] carriage – [Eisenbahn-] Wagen)

The teacher **coached** his students **in** mathematics. Coach: verb. (Solution: to teach – unterrichten in)

How to read non-fictional texts

Non-fictional or non-literary texts comprise various kinds of text, many of which are not normally chosen for use in English classes, e.g. documents, literary criticism, reviews, dictionary entries, forms, lists, instructions, descriptions, minutes, brochures, etc.
Text types such as expository texts, reports and argumentative texts, however, are of great importance in school.

All the non-fictional and literary texts in this chapter are about:
"Aggression and violence – Living in today's society".

Aggression: spoken or physical behaviour which is threatening or involving harm to somebody
Violence: actions or words which are intended to hurt people, often by extreme force
Crime: an action which is against the law or unacceptable

Expository texts

Expository texts describe a situation, a (technical) process, scientific findings, historic occurrences, etc. by presenting facts. The structure pattern of those texts is called topical order: A sequence of points follows a statement of the topic at the beginning of the text.

Before reading (P)

- In order to find out what the text may be about look at the title, the first sentence(s), pictures, diagrams, words in bold type, etc. You will get a rough idea of the content which leads you through the text.
- Think about what you would like to learn from the text.
- If possible, apply your background knowledge of the topic to the text.

While reading (R)

- Read the text carefully.
- Try to find out the relevant points and what you want to learn from the text.

- Mark the important parts of the text and note down key words for them in the margin.

After reading (R)

- Go back to the key words, read the sentences belonging to them again and note down the information in a table, diagram or mind map. (→ Mind map, p. 43)
- If you want or need further details, look them up in a specialised book or on the Internet.
- Talk about the text in class.

Example

Anthony Storr ◆ What is aggression?

When you read the text for the first time ignore the markings in the text and the notes in the margin.

Margin notes: different meanings of the term aggression – 1) 2) 3) 4) 5) 6)

To write about human aggression is a difficult task because the term is used in so many different senses. Aggression is one of those words which everyone knows, but which is nevertheless hard to define. As psychologists and psychiatrists use it, it covers a very wide range of human behaviour. 1) The red-faced infant squalling for the bottle is being aggressive; and so is 2) the judge who awards a thirty-year sentence for robbery. The 3) guard in a concentration camp who tortures his helpless victim is obviously acting aggressively. Less manifestly[1], but no less certainly, so is the 4) neglected wife who threatens or attempts suicide in order to regain her husband's affection. When a word becomes so diffusely applied that it is used both of the 5) competitive striving of a footballer and also of 6) the bloody violence of a murderer, it ought either to be dropped or else more closely defined. Aggression is a portmanteau term[2] which is fairly bursting at its seams[3]. Yet, until we can more clearly designate[4] and comprehend the various aspects of human behaviour which are subsumed under this head, we cannot discard[5] the concept.

Margin notes: aspects of aggression – 1) 2)

One difficulty is that there is no clear dividing line between those forms of aggression which we all deplore[6] and those which we must not disown if we are to survive. 1) When a child rebels against authority it is being aggressive: but it is also manifesting a drive[7] towards independence which is a necessary and valuable part of growing up. The 2) desire for power has, in extreme form, disastrous aspects which we all acknowledge: but the drive to conquer difficulties, or to gain mastery over the external world, underlies the greatest of human achievements.

[1] **manifest** clear and obvious – [2] **portmanteau term** word that combines two meanings – [3] **to burst at the seams** *aus allen Nähten platzen* – [4] **to designate** to point out sth. clearly – [5] **to discard** to stop using sth. – [6] **to deplore** *beklagen* – [7] **drive** desire to satisfy a need

Solution

Before and while reading

- The title is very expressive and clear: you can expect that the text will give a more comprehensive answer to the question "What is aggression?" than the definition in the box on page 17.
- The important parts of the text have been marked, headings for the different parts have been written in the margin.

After reading

The result of the analysis can be summed up like this:

Different meanings of the term aggression	
– baby crying for bottle of milk … – judge in court awarding a sentence … – guard in concentration camp … – neglected wife threatening to commit suicide … – footballer competing … – murderer …	… is aggressive

Negative and positive aspects of aggression

example	negative	positive
child's rebellion against authority	aggressive behaviour	striving for independence
man's desire for power	(in extreme form) disastrous	drive to conquer difficulties

- Discuss your results in class and collect additional examples. For further information see the text "Fox-hunting – for and against", pp. 24–25.

… And now it's your turn

Apply the foregoing reading technique to this text. Mark the relevant points and summarise your findings in a table or flow chart. (Flow chart: here a diagram which shows the ideas or topics of a text from top to bottom → example, p. 96)

Your notes

Anthony Storr ◆ Violence in early childhood

Most of the games which children play have an obvious aggressive content. Cops and robbers, cowboys and Indians, are examples of struggles in which the child, identifying itself with one or other side, is tempting to prove that it has some power in the world, some strength with which it can overcome the obstacles[1] which confront it.
Some adults, anxious that their children shall not grow into warmongers[2], proscribe the use of toy weapons, and discourage[3] games in which mock fighting plays a part. It is arguable that by doing so they are more likely to create the very type of personality which they are concerned to avoid. As Dr. Winicott has said: "If society is in danger, it is not because of man's aggressiveness but because of the repression of personal aggressiveness in individuals." The child's consciousness of its weakness compared with adults compels it to take every opportunity to prove its strength. In adult life it is the strong who least need to assert[4] themselves; but every child has to learn that it will not always remain in the weakest position and that it has at least some strength vis-à-vis other people.

[1] **to overcome obstacles** to defeat difficulties – [2] **warmonger** person who makes war – [3] **to discourage** to take away – [4] **to assert oneself** *sich behaupten*

Reports

A **report**, e.g. a newspaper report, informs the reader objectively about what happened somewhere. It gives answers to all or most of the six questions: Who?, What?, Where?, When?, Why? and How? and often gives further details. (Who did what, when, where, why and how?) Reports sometimes do not only consist of dry facts but are made livelier by fictional elements, e.g. by a detailed description of people and places or the way people are affected by the event.
News stories are a narrative variant of news reports. They narrate events in a subjective way and often want to entertain the reader.

Before reading (P)

- Read headline and subtitles first and have a look at pictures, diagrams, etc. What do they reveal about the content of the report?
- Have you heard anything about the news before? What would you like to read in this report?

While reading (R)

- Read the text carefully.
- Mark the information that answers the w- and h-questions, and note down the respective question words in the margin.

After reading (R)

- Go back to the interrogative words, read the sentences belonging to them again and organise the answers to the questions in key words in a diagram (→ p. 41) or mind map (→ p. 43) or enter them in a chart like this:

Who ______________________

did what, ______________________

when, ______________________

where, ______________________

why, ______________________

and how? ______________________

Further details: ______________________

- Talk about the report in class, especially about your views on the case and what has especially affected you.

Example

When you read the text for the first time ignore the markings in the text and the notes in the margin.

Another attack on the river

Mary R., an eighteen year old student, was attacked and brutally mistreated on her way home from a party on Saturday night. She had spent the evening with a friend of hers a few miles from her home. She left at 11 p.m. because she didn't want to be home too late. She took a short-cut along the river-bank. Suddenly she heard footsteps and began to run. But the man behind her was quicker. He caught up with her and snatched her handbag. Luckily, a car was passing by when the man was about to rape her. He grabbed her and knocked her head against a tree. It was absolutely horrible. The young woman screamed and prayed for God to help her. The driver stopped and went to help the woman while the man ran away. Mary R. reported the man to the police the next morning. She described him as tall, red-haired, about twenty and wearing blue jeans and a leather jacket. The police officer took down the details of the case and then said to her: "We'll do our best to find the man. You had a narrow escape but it might be worse next time. Don't walk alone after dark again."

What?
When?
Where?
Who?
How?
Further details
Who?
Further details

Solution

Before reading

- The headline and the first sentence supply you with the information about the content of the text: the text will be about an attack on a young woman on her way home.
- You may have heard about attacks on teenagers and young women and are curious about what happened this time.

While reading

- You may underline the important pieces of information and jot down the respective question words in the margin (see text).

After reading

- You may summarise your findings in a mind map:

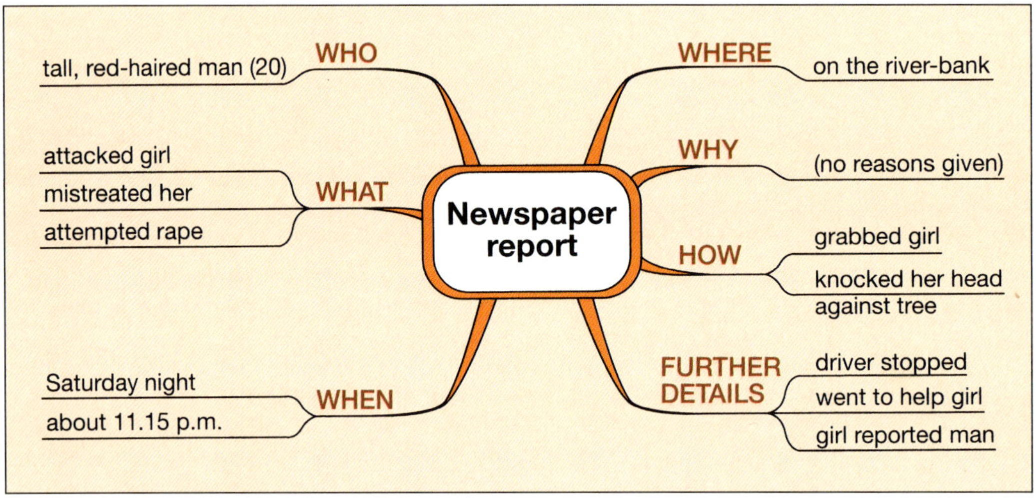

… And now it's your turn

Apply the foregoing reading technique to the following text, underline the most important points and summarise your findings in a mind map.

Your notes ↓

Troops on full alert as bomb left outside prison 29th April 2002

Police and troops in Northern Ireland are on full alert after a failed bomb attack on a high security prison. It has emerged that a vehicle used to transport a bomb was left outside Maghaberry Jail, near Lisburn, Co Antrim. The detonator exploded, but the bomb – weighing nearly 150lb – did not go off.

Dissident republicans opposed to the peace process have been blamed

for the attack. The explosion occurred at a perimeter gate, usually manned by staff who check identification of the people coming into the jail. A two-minute warning was given, allowing a full evacuation of the area. Around 700 prison officers and up to 500 prisoners are housed in the complex. Detectives in Lisburn say the scene is cordoned off and are appealing for witnesses and information. On Friday, police in Belfast intercepted a van bomb which they believe was going to be left outside the offices of the Ulster Unionist Party near the city centre.
The white Mitsubishi four-wheel-drive vehicle abandoned with the bomb at Maghaberry last night was stolen in Dublin a fortnight ago.

A senior security source said: "Security has been heightened at all police and military bases. Even before Friday, we knew they (the dissidents) were planning something major."

Argumentative texts

Argumentative texts, written or spoken, deal with controversial topics. The reasons advanced for or against the matter under discussion are arranged in a calculated order with the purpose of convincing the reader or listener.

Argumentative texts normally fall into three parts:

a) Introduction: Presenting a topic and giving opinions on the problem.

b) Main part: Supporting them by arguments (type 1), sometimes also giving counter-arguments and refuting them in order to stress the author's position (type 2) or in a dispute between two speakers a steady change of arguments and counter-arguments (type 3, dialectic method).

c) Conclusion: Presenting a solution to the problem and/or predicting certain consequences.

Forms of argumentative texts

Type 1	Type 2	Type 3 (mainly in disputes and debates)
Introduction	Introduction	Introduction
Arguments	Arguments	Argument Counter-argument Argument Counter-argument
Supporting facts	Counter-arguments and refutation	
Conclusion	Conclusion	Conclusion

Before reading (P)

- Read the heading and words in bold type first and find out what the text will deal with.
- What knowledge about the topic do you already have? It will help you to understand the text.

While reading (R)

- Mark the most important information.
  Read difficult texts twice before taking notes.
- **Introduction** Find out the writer's topic and his opinion.
- **Main part** Find out the form of argumentation first. Then mark arguments and possible counter-arguments. Number the arguments and counter-arguments in the margin and show how they are connected.
- **Conclusion** What conclusion does the writer/speaker draw? Underline it in the text.

After reading (R)

- Go back to the text and your notes in the margin and summarise the author's argumentation (→ Summary, p. 55) or fill in a chart.
- The aim of argumentative texts is to convince the reader to share the writer's or speaker's opinion. Has this purpose been achieved? Are the arguments put forward convincing?

Example

When you read the text for the first time ignore the markings in the text and the notes in the margin.

Christopher Cortis, Desmond Clayton ◆ Fox-hunting[1] – for and against

Introduction→ **Main part↓** argument 1

CORTIS. Fox-hunting is one of those things which most people are pretty clearly "for" or "against". Those in favour are often somewhat surprised when asked to defend their favourite sport: hunting seems to them such a natural thing that it hardly requires any defending. […]

counter-argument

CLAYTON. My objection to fox-hunting is that it is a long-drawn-out torture imposed by so-called thinking animals on a very intelligent animal. Above all, it is a very sensitive beast. I simply think that a torture imposed like this solely for the pleasure of another animal is wrong.

argument 2

CORTIS. It may well be morally wrong – or be considered by many people to be morally wrong. But this doesn't make it something to be prohibited[2] by law. Morals are not the province of law. Law is there to safeguard society – and fox-hunting does not endanger society.

counter-argument

CLAYTON. I think it does, on a long-term view. It brutalises those engaged in it – or makes them more brutal than they already are, which cannot do society any good in the long run. It hides primitive instincts, which should be sublimated[3] in any kind of civilised society. […]

I can suggest a number: for example team games. I think team games provide a very suitable outlet for this desire for a primitive thrill – and they also satisfy the need for physical exercise. The question, for me, is simply whether man should be allowed to behave like a bloodthirsty animal. […]

CORTIS. But man is a bloodthirsty animal, and like any other animal he must find some way of satisfying his bloodthirsty instincts. And I have a feeling, after having listened to some of the statements made by fox-hunting people, that they are the sort of people who might, if they don't hunt foxes, hunt other people. There's no question, I think, that it's more civilised to let them get rid of their pent-up[4] aggressions on the fox rather than on their fellow-men.

argument 3

CLAYTON. Yes, but is this really necessary? They may need an outlet for their pent-up aggressions, but if there is a way of providing this outlet without being cruel to animals, then this makes blood sports unnecessary.

counter-argument

CORTIS. You know, I seriously doubt if there is a really adequate substitute for fox-hunting as practised in Britain.

argument 4

CLAYTON. And I doubt whether a society that does not educate people to the extent where they no longer need the thrill of killing an animal can really be called civilised. Now to close this session, I'd like to ask you to sum up.

counter-argument

CORTIS. Gladly. Summing up, I think we can say that the case against fox-hunting was based on the view that it is society's responsibility to prevent cruelty to animals by legal means if necessary. The case for fox-hunting was based on the submission[5] that it provides a necessary outlet for aggression, and also that we have no right in a liberal society to legislate against other people's private pleasures.

Conclusion

[1] **fox-hunting** see description pp. 12–13 – [2] **to prohibit** to forbid by law, rule, etc. – [3] **to sublimate** to modify into a culturally higher activity – [4] **pent-up** held back, repressed – [5] **submission** here: belief, assumption

Solution

Before reading (P)

- The title and the names (Cortis and Clayton) suggest that the text will deal with a dispute about fox-hunting between these two men.
- Fox-hunting is popular in many countries, especially in Britain, and you are anxious to learn what the reasons for and against fox-hunting will be.

While reading (R)

- In the text above the most important reasons for and against fox-hunting have been marked and numbered in the margin. Cortis is for and Clayton against fox-hunting.

After reading (R)

- The form of argumentation is type 3, a chart may look look this:

Introduction (statement)
Fox-hunting is one of those sports which people are for and against.

Main part

Argument 1: Fox-hunting: a natural kind of sport	Counter-argument: Fox-hunting: a torture of animals for the pleasure of man
Argument 2: Fox-hunting does not endanger society, it does not have to be prohibited.	Counter-argument: Fox-hunting brutalises people, it's a danger to society. Primitive instincts have to be sublimated, e.g. by team games.
Argument 3: Man a bloodthirsty being, should get rid of pent-up aggressions on the fox rather than on fellow-men.	Counter-argument: Outlet for pent-up aggressions without being cruel to animals
Argument 4: There is no adequate substitute for fox-hunting.	Counter-argument: People who need the thrill of killing an animal can't be called civilised.

Conclusion (summary of both views)
For fox-hunting: Necessary outlet for pent-up aggressions
Against fox-hunting: Cruelty to animals

Evaluation: your position

- You may think that Christopher Cortis has most probably not persuaded his listeners or readers to accept his view.
  His arguments are rather weak, they are only based on the idea that man is a bloodthirsty being and that there is no other outlet for his aggressive behaviour than fox-hunting.

... And now it's your turn

Apply the foregoing reading technique to the following text, mark the relevant points and summarise your findings in a chart.

George Orwell ◆ Serious sport is war minus the shooting

Your notes ↓

I am always amazed when I hear people saying that sport creates goodwill between the nations, and that if only the common people of the world could meet one another at football or cricket, they would have no inclination to meet on the battlefield. Even if one didn't know from concrete examples that international sporting contests lead to orgies of hatred, one could deduce it from general principles.

Nearly all the sports practised nowadays are competitive. You play to win, and the game has little meaning unless you do your utmost to win. On the village green, where no feeling of local patriotism is involved, it is possible to play simply for the fun and exercise: but as soon as the question of prestige arises, as soon as you feel that you and some larger unit will be disgraced if you lose, the most savage combative instincts are aroused. Anyone who has played even in a school football match knows this.

At the international level sport is frankly mimic warfare. But the significant thing is not the behaviour of the players but the attitude of the spectators; and, behind the spectators, of the nations who work themselves into furies over these absurd contests, and seriously believe – at any rate for short periods – that running, jumping and kicking a ball are tests of national virtue.

As soon as strong feelings of rivalry are aroused, the notion of playing the game according to the rules always vanishes. People want to see one side on top and the other side humiliated[1] and they forget that victory gained through cheating or through the intervention[2] of the crowd is meaningless. Even when the spectators don't intervene[3] physically they try to influence the game by cheering their own side and "rattling" opposing players with hatred, jealousy, boastfulness, disregard of all rules and sadistic pleasure in witnessing violence: in other words it is war minus the shooting.

[1] **to humiliate** to make feel ashamed – [2] **intervention** action to improve a situation – [3] **to intervene** to prevent sth. from being done, to come between

How to read fictional texts

Prose fiction

The **elements of prose fiction** (short stories and novels) are characters (persons in a fictional text), setting (the time and place at which events take place), action (everything that happens), theme (central idea) and plot (series of events). Actions may be external, when the writer describes what the characters do and/or say, or they may be internal, when the writer shows the thoughts and feelings of the characters.
The action in short stories is brief; they deal with one main event or conflict whereas novels are more complicated.

Understanding and analysing a short story

Before reading (P)

Expectations and predictions

- Before starting to read you should have a close look at pictures, the title and the beginning of the text and ask yourself what it may be about. Your expectations and predictions arouse your interest in the text and guide you while reading it.
- Ask yourself questions that you would like to be answered by the text: How may the situation develop, how will the characters behave, etc.?

While reading (R)

Reading intensively or extensively

- When you need to understand as many details as possible, e.g. at the beginning of a text, read slowly and carefully.
  When you want to get just a general impression of the text or the main points, you can skim over it and ignore irrelevant passages.
  (→ Extensive and intensive reading techniques, p. 12)
- When you start reading pay attention to the beginning of the text: the presentation of situation, characters, setting, etc. Read it in detail in order to get a good basis for understanding the whole text.
- Follow the course of action, the plot.
- You may experience that the development of the action does not come up to what you have expected. Stop once in a while, and change your predictions based on what you have just read and guess how the action might go on.

- Pay special attention to key events.

> The way the action is structured so that suspense is created (growing feeling of excitement that makes a reader curious about the outcome of a story) is called plot.
> A **plot** has normally several stages: exposition (introduction to the main characters, the setting, etc.), rising action (developing conflict), climax (the moment when the conflict is most intense), turning point (the point at which an important change takes place), falling action (reduction in suspense) and resolution (solution to the problem).

- It is very helpful for full understanding of a long narrative text and later discussion in class to jot down notes in the margin of your textbook (elements of the story: characters, setting, plot) or to keep a reading log.
- Put down keywords after finishing a chapter or at an appropriate moment while reading the text.

A **reading log** is a reader's record of thoughts. It should have two columns.

Elements of the text:	Response to the text:
↓	↓
characters	impressions
setting	questions/problems
(key) events	speculations
…	points for discussion
	…

Respective pages/lines have to be given for all entries.

After reading (R)

- Go over your notes or entries in the reading log and read relevant passages again.
- Make a diagram like this and note down the points you would like to discuss in class:

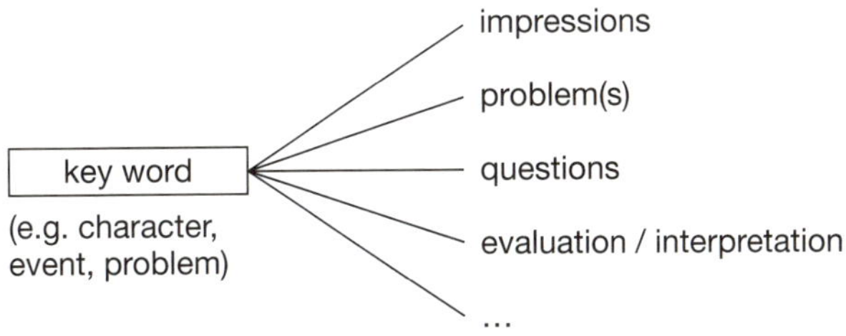

- You may want to analyse the style in which the text is written and find out how it contributes to understanding the story. (→ Style, p. 67)

Example

When you read the story for the first time ignore the notes in the margin.

Dennis Kurumada ◆ Just along for the ride

Margin notes ↓

setting

I leaned back on the seat and watched the back of Dick's head as he steered. The '55 DeSoto rumbled along the rain-soaked street.

This evening's gonna be a total loss, I thought. Things have gotta be pretty dull when all you've got to do is drive around with a friend who just got his licence. But it beats sitting home.

characters situation

So there we were, five of us. Dick and Phil were in front. Reid, Steve, and I were in the back. We were all cold, damp, and bored. Man, we needed something to do!

"This is really crummy[1]. I think we …"

I was cut off by Phil. "Hey, let's drive up to somebody … some kid … and flatten him."

"What?" I said.

plan to kill time: driving around and hitting a person

"We drive up slow, then swing open the door real fast, and knock the guy on his can."

We all looked at him kinda[2] funny.

"Well, it's something to do," Phil said.

"Aw, why not? Okay, we'll do it."

We began looking around for a victim.

"You guys are nuts[3]", I said. "What if he calls the cops?"

"You worry too much. Whenever we wanna have some fun, you always chicken out[4]."

"There's one!"

It was raining hard, but we could see the blurred figure of some guy under a streetlight on the corner. Steve laughed.

spotting a victim for plan

"Oh wow! This is gonna be funny."

A couple of us started laughing.

"Will you guys shut up?" said Dick. I guess it made him nervous.

The kid was about half a block away. The street wasn't too busy. Only a few cars were around. Dick started weaving[5] across the road.

"Stop fooling around!" I said.

Steve got on the door, ready to open it. Then everything started happening too fast. The guy at the corner stepped out into the street. The car swerved. The door swung open, and Steve started falling out. He grabbed my arm, and we both fell back on the seat.

Dick got scared and threw the car away from the kid. The headlights flashed on a frozen figure. I could see his face, eyes wide, mouth open. There was a squeal of tires on the slick[6] street and a hollow thud as the figure was hurled, rolling across the roof. I got all mixed up.

↓ carrying out plan, accident

"Ken Benjamin!" I said. "I think that was Ken Benjamin!"

Dick slowed down. Then he suddenly started speeding down the street.

"Dick! Stop! I know that guy! Dick, will ya stop?" He didn't hear me.

"Stop the car! He's my friend!"

I hit him on the shoulder and grabbed his shirt. He turned around. Tears were blobbing up in his eyes.

"Shut up, you jerk! You want us to get nailed for man-slaughter?" He hit my arm. What a stupid thing to do!

↓ hit and run

I got so scared that I started shivering like crazy. I just couldn't believe it. I felt sick.

"Hey!"

I looked up. It was Dick. He was looking in the rearview mirror. There was a car behind us.

"Is he following us?" I asked.

"Well, I'll lose him," said Dick.

The car lunged forward as it picked up speed. I looked back. The headlights shone through the rain, about two or three hundred yards away. Dick hung a sharp right up a narrow street.

Hardly anyone ever comes up this way, I thought. If he follows us up here, he's really following us. I looked back. The headlights were even closer. We started up a winding road. I looked back and could see the brown Volvo as it cut through the street ponds. Yeah, I thought, a good guy would drive one of those Volvos. What if he catches us?

Ken was my friend. *Hit and run, hit and run*[7] kept going through my head. I kinda hoped that guy would catch us.

We were out in the sticks by now. The roads were winding a lot. The Volvo was making his move, and was closing fast. But as he rounded a curve, he turned too sharply and his car slid off the road. He couldn't have been hurt. Every one was relieved. After that, Dick drove us all home.

It was 12:30 when I got home. Nobody was awake. I started pacing around the kitchen. I was so scared. I didn't know if we had killed him or not. I turned on the radio and listened to some music.

↓ relief

But when the news came on, I turned it off. You idiot, I thought. Ken was your friend. Go to his mom or something. Well, I didn't hit him! It's not my fault! Those other guys … it wasn't my idea … no! You were in the car. You're responsible, too. *Hit and run, hit and run.*

I got in my car and drove for a while. Then I started remembering things Ken used to say.

"I don't know what to do!" I was shouting as I drove. No answer. My mind burned. "Go see Mrs. Benjamin, you coward!"

But I couldn't. I just couldn't. When I got home, the lights were on. My mother was in her robe. "Your friends are here," she said. "I don't think that two o'clock in the morning is the right time to …"

I didn't listen. I just went into the front room. Dick walked up to me and said real low, "I heard on the radio that he's not dead. He isn't even hurt bad."

victim not dead I didn't say anything. I just looked at him.

"No one knows," he went on. "So maybe we can get away with it."

He could see I was getting mad. I could have killed him.

The others stood up and came over. I didn't say a thing. I just walked out the door, got in the car, and left.

It took me a while to find Ken's house. It was gray brick, and the lights were on. Maybe it wasn't gray.

I don't know. Everything looked gray. I walked up and rang the doorbell.

[1] **crummy** boring – [2] **kinda** somewhat – [3] **nuts** crazy – [4] **to chicken out** to become cowardly – [5] **to weave** to move along, changing direction frequently – [6] **slick** slippery – [7] **hit and run** *Fahrerflucht*

Solution

Before reading (P)

- The picture shows a group of teenagers. They seem to be bored. The title and the first paragraph suggest that they will kill time by driving around. The prediction is that something strange will happen. But what?

While reading (R)

- The prediction that something strange will happen proves to be true (ll. 5–18). But the question is: will Phil really carry out his plan "to drive up to somebody and flatten him" (ll. 10f.) and how will the first person narrator of the story behave (→ Point of view, p. 77), questions that guide further reading.
- Intensive and extensive reading follow one another, e.g. the introduction to the story (ll. 1–15) or key stages in the plot (e.g. ll. 28ff.) require detailed reading whereas other passages (e.g. ll. 57ff.) can be read quickly.
- Margin notes: see text above

Reading log:

Elements of the text	Response to the text
Characters (ll. 6f.): Dick, Phil, Reid, Steve, narrator	
Setting (ll. 2f.) • teenagers in a '55 DeSoto on a rain-soaked street • evening	
Plot (key events): • teenagers bored, plan to kill time: driving up to sb. and hitting him (ll. 13f.)	plan abominable
• spotting and chasing a victim (ll. 23ff.) • accident (ll. 35ff.)	unexpected accident
• hit-and-run driving (ll. 62) • at the narrator's home, relief (l. 83)	points for discussion in class: see diagram below

After reading (R)

- The diagram shows the points that may be suggested for discussion in class:

Crime for fun
- moral consideration
- social problem
- characters' attitude towards criminal act: regret?
- question: why open ending?

- Summary of the points that could be put forward:

	Phil	other boys	narrator
introduction	knocking sb. over: opportunity of killing time	unanimous approval	doubts, fear of police
after accident	fear of police, calm again after radio news		guilt-ridden, inner conflict

- The author uses a lot of irregularities of language and slang expressions, e.g. "evening gonna be", "kinda", "you guys are nuts", "out in the sticks", "to chicken out", etc. He makes his characters speak in this way because he wants to show that the boys belong to a group and that the group uses certain informal expressions and slang to give itself a kind of special identity.

Drama

A **play (or drama)** is a piece of literature that is written to be presented on a stage. Actors and actresses play the roles of the characters. A full-length play is divided into acts and scenes. A short play is a one-act play that is not divided into smaller parts. In every play you will find elements as in a short story: theme, setting, characters and plot.

… And now it's your turn

Apply the foregoing reading technique to the following scene from Yamauchi's play "And the soul shall dance". Make notes in the margin and summarise your suggestions for a discussion in a mind map.

Wakaho Yamauchi ◆ And the soul shall dance

The action takes place in Southern California.
Two Japanese families, the Murata and Oka family, struggle for a better life in America. Murata's daughter, Masako, and Oka's newly arrived daughter, Kiyoko, establish a relationship. In this scene, Masako and Kiyoko engage in a small battle of culture and language.

> **Stage directions** are notes in a play that tell the actors how to speak and act. They also say what the characters and the stage should look like and where and when the action takes place.
> Stage directions also help the reader, who cannot see the play performed on stage, to get a vivid idea of what is going on.

Characters: Masako, 12, Kiyoko, 14

The Murata house and yard. Masako prepares to go to school. She puts on a coat and picks up her books and lunch bag. Meanwhile, Kiyoko slips quietly into the yard. Masako walks out and is surprised to see Kiyoko.

Your notes ↓

Masako: Hi. I thought you'd be … sick today.
Kiyoko: Oh. I woke up late.
Masako: *(Scrutinizing[1] Kiyoko's face)* Your eyes are red.
Kiyoko: *(Averting[2] her eyes)* Oh. I … got … sand in it. Yes.
Masako: Do you want to use eye drops? We have eye drops in the house.
Kiyoko: Oh … no. That's all right.
Masako: That's what you call bloodshot.
Kiyoko: Oh …
Masako: My father gets it a lot. When he drinks too much.
Kiyoko: Oh …
Masako: *(Notices Kiyoko doesn't have her lunch.)* Where's your lunch bag?
Kiyoko: I … forgot it.
Masako: Did you make your lunch today?
Kiyoko: Yes. Yes, I did. But I forgot it.
Masako: Do you want to go back and get it?

Kiyoko: No, that's all right. *(They are silent for a while.)* We'll be late.

Masako: Do you want to practice your words?

Kiyoko: *(Thoughtfully.)* Oh …

Masako: Say, "My."

Kiyoko: My?

Masako: Eyes …

Kiyoko: Eyes.

Masako: Are …

Kiyoko: Are.

Masako: Red.

Kiyoko: Red.

Masako: Your eyes are red. *(Kiyoko doesn't repeat it)* I … *(Kiyoko doesn't co-operate.)* Say, "I."

Kiyoko: I.

Masako: Got …

Kiyoko: Got.

Masako: Sand … *(Kiyoko balks[3].)* Say, "I."

Kiyoko: *(Sighing.)* I.

Masako: Reft …

Kiyoko: Reft.

Masako: My …

Kiyoko: My.

Masako: Runch …

Kiyoko: Run … lunch. *(She stops.)* Masako-san, you are mean. You are hurting me.

Masako: It's a joke! I was just trying to make you laugh!

Kiyoko: I cannot laugh today.

Masako: Sure you can. You can laugh. Laugh! Like this. *(She makes a hearty laugh.)*

Kiyoko: I cannot laugh when you make fun of me.

Masako: Okay, I'm sorry. We'll practice some other words then, okay? *Kiyoko doesn't answer.)* Say, "Okay."

Kiyoko: *(Reluctantly.)* Okay …

Masako: Okay, then … um … um … *(She still teases and talks rapidly.)* Say … um … "She sells sea shells on the seashore." *(Kiyoko turns away indignantly[4].)* Aw, come on, Kiyoko! It's just a joke. Laugh!

Kiyoko: *(Imitating sarcastically.)* Ha-ha-ha! Now you say, "Kono kyaku wa yoku kaki ku kyaku da [This guest eats a lot of persimmons]!"

Masako: Sure! I can say it! Kono kyaku waki ku kyoku kaku …

Kiyoko: That's not right.

Masako: Koki kuki kya …

Kiyoko: No.

Masako: Okay, then. You say, "Sea sells she shells … shu … sss …" *(They both laugh, Kiyoko with her hands over her mouth. Masako takes Kiyokos's hands from her mouth.)* Not like that! Like this! *(She gives a big belly laugh.)*

Kiyoko: Like this? *(She imitates Masako.)*

Masako: Yeah, that's right! You're not mad anymore?

Kiyoko: I'm not mad anymore.

Masako: Okay. You can share my lunch today because we're …

Kiyoko: "Flends?"

[1] **to scrutinize** to look at, to exame carefully – [2] **to avert** to turn away – [3] **to balk** *stocken, stutzen* – [4] **indignant** angry and scornful

Poetry

A **poem** can normally be identified by formal features such as stanza, verse, rhyme, rhythm or metre (except in free verse poems). Poetic language tends to differ from everyday language; it is often concentrated and more obscure than that of prose.
Most poems have two levels: the level of exterior meaning (level of mere description) and the level of interior meaning (level of deeper meaning).

Before reading (P)

- Look at the title and think about the possible meaning it holds; poets often choose rather vague headings that invite the reader to speculate.

While reading (R)

Guidelines for reading a poem: a three step method

Step 1 1. The content of the poem

- Read the poem once slowly aloud without writing or marking anything. Note down your first impression in one or two sentences.
- Read the poem again silently word by word, if necessary several times. Look up words you don't know, paraphrase lines that seem to be obscure in order to have a fairly good idea of the content of the poem.
- Jot down some notes about the content.

Step 2 2. The form of the poem

- Study the poem for formal aspects and stylistic devices (cf. box below) which the poet uses to convey his message to the reader.

alliteration: the repetition of consonants at the beginning of neighbouring words in order to stress them, e.g. round the rocks runs the river

assonance: the repetition of the same vowel within two or more words as a means of accentuation, e.g. sharper – garter

rhyme: the repetition of sounds at the end of two or more lines or in the middle of a poem's lines, e.g. full rhyme: show – blow; eye rhyme: dies – stories

rhyme scheme: the pattern created by rhymes, e.g. rhyming couplets: aabbcc …, alternate rhyme: ababcdcd …, embracing rhyme: abba cddc

rhythm: the regular or irregular stress pattern in a line of a poem

metre: the pattern of stressed (/) and unstressed (◡) syllables in a line of a poem, e.g. iambic metre: ◡/; trochaic metre: /◡; free verse: no fixed metre. The type of metre chosen by the poet gives the poem a certain rhythm and stresses important words or ideas.

metaphor: an indirect comparison of two different objects or ideas. Metaphors suggest a likeness between two words without using 'like' or 'as', e.g. the river of life

parallelism: the repetition of parts of a sentence to stress elements of equal importance

personification: type of figurative language in which human qualities are attributed to an object, animal or idea, e.g. treating love as a person

repetition: repeating words or ideas in order to emphasise individual phrases or sentences or to focus attention

simile: a direct comparison between two different objects or ideas indicated by 'like' or 'as' in order to achieve greater expressiveness, e.g. her lips are as red as roses

symbol: an object, a character or an event that stands for an abstract idea in order to create complex associations, e.g. the cross for Christianity, the rose for love

see also "Previews" p 109 /

- Think of the effect these devices may have on the deeper meaning of the poem.
  Ask yourself questions like: 'Why did the poet choose …?'

3. Content + form = meaning

Step 3

- In your notes, make final comments on the way the poem's content and form work together to create the deeper, more general meaning. What is the poet's overall message?

After reading (R)

- Think of how the poem affects you. Give examples to show what you mean.
- Do you find anything particularly interesting or confusing in the poem?

Example

Read this poem and follow the pattern given above.

William Soutar ◆ The children

Upon the street they lie
Beside the broken stone:
The blood of children stares from the broken stone.

Death came out of the sky
In the bright afternoon:
Darkness slanted[1] over the bright afternoon.

Again the sky is clear
But upon earth a stain[2]
The earth is darkened with a darkening stain.

A wound which everywhere
Corrupts[3] the hearts of men:
The blood of children corrupts the hearts of men.

Silence is in the air:
The stars move to their places:
Silent and serene[4] the stars move to their places.

But from the earth the children stare
With blind and fearful faces:
And our charity[5] is in the children's faces.

[1] **to slant** to lean – [2] **stain** dirty patch of colour – [3] **to corrupt** to cause to change from good to bad – [4] **serene** calm and peaceful – [5] **charity** sympathy and kindness

Solution

Before reading (P)

- The title is rather vague. It is not before the end of the first stanza that predictions about the content of the poem can be made: it will probably refer to children in war.

While reading (R)

Step 1 1. The content of the poem

- The first response could be: Feelings of compassion and pity for the innocent victims of the bomb attack.
- Words which will probably be unknown and have to be looked up are: to slant, stain, serene, and charity.
- Content. Your notes: The poem describes the disastrous effects of a bomb attack, the destruction of a city and the death of its population. The focus is on the most innocent victims of war, the children. The attack unexpectedly strikes a formerly harmonious world.

Step 2 2. The form of the poem

The poet employs various devices to modify literal meaning:

device	example	meaning / function
metaphor	darkness (l. 6)	the shadow cast by the bombers, but also the disaster and misery that war entails
	silence (l. 13)	the real silence after the bomb attack as all life has been destroyed, but also the lack of human emotions
symbol (imagery, metaphors)	broken stone (ll. 2, 3) blood (ll. 3, 12) stain (ll. 8, 9)	a sign of destruction and devastation a sign of death a sign of guilt
personification	the blood of children stares/corrupts (ll. 3, 12)	the blood of the victims is like a person who accuses the soldiers who kill innocent people
repetition	children (ll. 3, 12, 16, 18)	emphasising that it is the children who are the real victims of war
	stain (ll. 8, 9)	reminding the reader of the fact that the soldiers have done wrong
	broken stone (ll. 2, 3)	stress on the result of the bomb attack
	stars (ll. 14, 15)	the stars symbolise the indifference of nature, the universe and the rest of the world towards the plight of a war's victims
alliteration	<u>d</u>arkened with a <u>d</u>arkening stain (l. 9)	emphasis on the dark (disastrous) result of the bomb attack
metre	Upon the street they lie Beside the broken stone: The blood of children stares from the broken stone.	The regular iambic metre at the beginning of the poem is soon broken to show the disturbed harmony in the city.

3. Content and form = meaning

Step 3

The poem describes the result of a bomb attack: the destruction of a city and the death of children.
The sudden change in metre at the beginning of the poem shows that the bomb attack unexpectedly destroys the peace of a formerly harmonious world.
The use of metaphors (darkness, silence: result of the aggressive act), symbols (broken stone, blood, stain: signs of destruction and death) and repetitions (children, blood of children: death of innocent young people) add to the description of the disastrous effects of the bomb attack.
The alliteration in combination with the repetition of the verb *darken* 'darkened with darkening stain' demonstrates the disastrous situation after the attack (darkened = destroyed life) but also shows that the bomb attack has a lasting effect and is creating a feeling of guilt (darkening stain: feeling guilty).
All the stylistic devices contribute to the poet's intention. Content and form taken together bring about the deeper meaning "Wars lead to harm and disaster and are inhumane". The poet's message is "Wars must be prevented".

... And now it's your turn

Apply the foregoing reading technique to this poem. Read the poem and follow the three step method: content, form and content + form = meaning.

Wilfred Owen ◆ Futility[1]

Move him into the sun –
Gently its touch awoke him once,
At home, whispering of fields unsown.
Always it woke him, even in France,
Until this morning and this snow.
If anything might rouse[2] him now
The kind old sun will know.

Think how it wakes the seeds, –
Woke, once, the clays[3] of a cold star.
Are limbs, so dear-achieved[4], are sides,
Full-nerved – still warm – too hard to stir?
Was it for this the clay grew tall?
– O what made fatuous[5] sunbeams toil[6]
To break earth's sleep at all?

[1] **futility** uselessness – [2] **to rouse** to bring out of sleep – [3] **clay** stiff sticky earth that becomes hard when baked (in Christian mythology God formed man out of clay) – [4] **to achieve** to reach sth. by skill – [5] **fatuous** foolish – [6] **to toil** to work hard

How to write – general writing skills

Writing a text

Writing texts is an important skill you need in school and also in real life. Good texts are well-planned and clearly structured. The writing process consists of the following steps: a) Gathering ideas, b) organising them and planning the text, c) writing a draft, d) revising the text, and e) writing a fair copy.

Important aspects

What you should always keep in mind:

Whenever you write a text, either in school or in real life, consider the following aspects:

- **WHO** am I writing this text for? (Reader/audience)
- **WHY** am I writing this text? (Purpose)
- **WHAT** do I want to say? (Content)
- **HOW** do I have to write the text? (Style, language, layout)

a) Gathering ideas and information

Before writing the draft

- Before you start writing, you may use these techniques for collecting ideas:
  - Brainstorming
  - Making a net diagram
  - Filling in a grid or note-making chart

Sources of information

- Sources for gathering ideas are texts or books you have read, films you have seen, personal experience, reference books, researches on the Internet, etc. (→ p. 9)

Brainstorming

- In brainstorming you concentrate on finding ideas for or a solution to a given problem task. You note down as many words and phrases as possible as they come to your mind without evaluating them. You do not have to arrange them in order of importance.

Example: Native Americans (brainstorming)

- minority, about two million
- in many parts of the USA
- poor living conditions
- many tribes and languages
- land nobody's property
- Europeans' materialistic view of earth and land
- Europeans brought diseases and alcohol
- peaceful, small communities
- Europeans' materialistic view of land
- nature-based religion
- Europeans exploited Indians
- Europeans destroyed Indian culture
- fighting for rights, recognition
- Indian wars, ended 1890
- 50% on reservations
- Indian beliefs, religion
- problems: unemployed, infertile land
- rest in villages, big cities
- Europeans created reservations
- Mother Earth sacred

- After you have finished brainstorming, check your findings and decide on what ideas you want to use.

Net diagram

- When using a net diagram for brainstorming purposes, write down your topic in the middle of a sheet of paper and circle it. From there draw lines at the end of which you note down a word or short phrase. You can draw more lines either from the key word in the middle or from other words you have jotted down.

Example: Native Americans (net diagram)

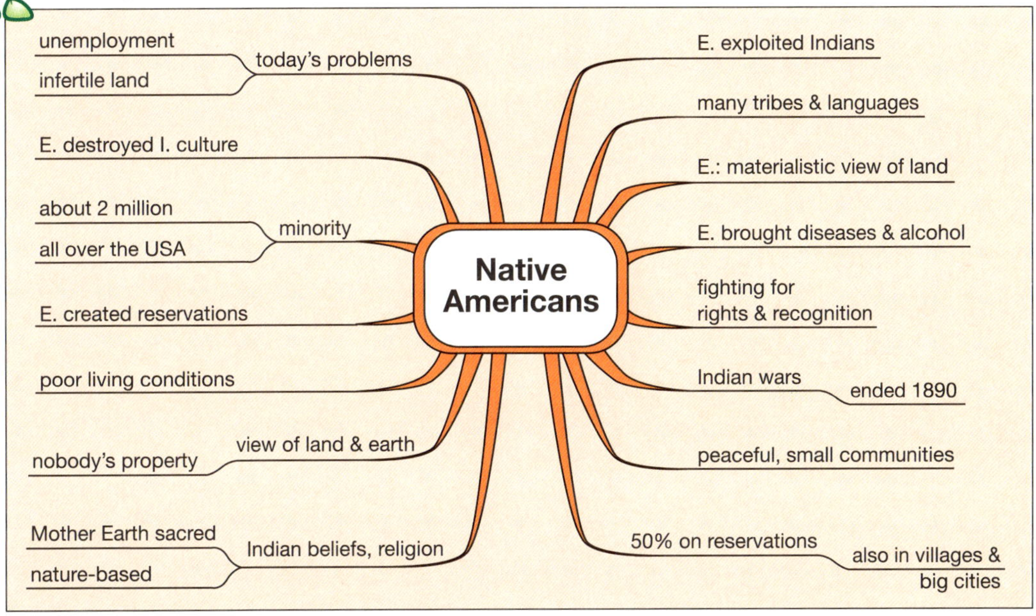

- After you have finished, check your results and cross out ideas you do not want to use.

Grid or note making-chart

- A grid or note-making chart is a diagram that consists of vertical and horizontal lines. The number of lines depends on the amount of headings you decide on. Mind that the columns are wide enough for your entries. A grid is used for gathering ideas under different headings. It is a useful method to help you pre-select ideas.

Example: Native Americans (grid/note-making chart)

Indian history	Europeans	Beliefs & religion	N. Americans today
• many tribes & languages • peaceful communities • Indian wars • many killed • 1890: end of wars	• materialistic view of land • brought diseases & alcohol • created reservations • destroyed Indian culture • exploited Indians	• Mother Earth sacred • land nobody's property • nature-based religion	• minority, two million • 50% on reservations • in villages & big cities • in many parts of the USA • poor living conditions • unemployment, infertile land, no farming and hunting • fighting for rights & recognition

b) Organising ideas and planning the text

- After you have collected enough ideas, it is important to organise them and plan your text carefully because you must have a clear idea of the content before you start to write.
- Decide on the ideas you are going to use for your text and plan your paragraphs.

Organising ideas by numbering them

- You may order your points by numbering them. This will help you to save time.

Example: Ordering brainstorming results (by numbering them)

- minority, about two million (12)
- in many parts of the USA (15)
- poor living conditions (16)
- many tribes and languages (2)
- land nobody's property (5)
- Europeans' materialistic view of earth and land (11)
- Europeans brought diseases and alcohol (7)
- peaceful, small communities (1)
- nature-based religion (6)
- Europeans exploited Indians (10)
- Europeans destroyed Indian culture (8)
- fighting for rights, recognition (18)
- Indian wars, ended 1890 (3)
- 50% on reservations (13)
- unemployment, infertile land, no farming and hunting (17)
- rest in villages, big cities (14)
- Europeans created reservations (9)
- Mother Earth sacred (4)

Mind maps and topic outlines will help you to order ideas in a more systematic way.

Using a mind map

- A mind map consists of a net-like web of linked ideas. When drawing a mind map, note down your topic in the middle of a sheet of paper and circle it. Then draw lines (branches) on which you write topic-related words or short phrases in capital letters. You can draw more lines either from a line you have drawn or from the key word in the middle. In a mind map ideas appear in hierarchical order, e.g. according to importance.

  Note: Mind maps are used for organising ideas. Net diagrams are used for collecting them in a spontaneous way.

Example: Native Americans (mind map)

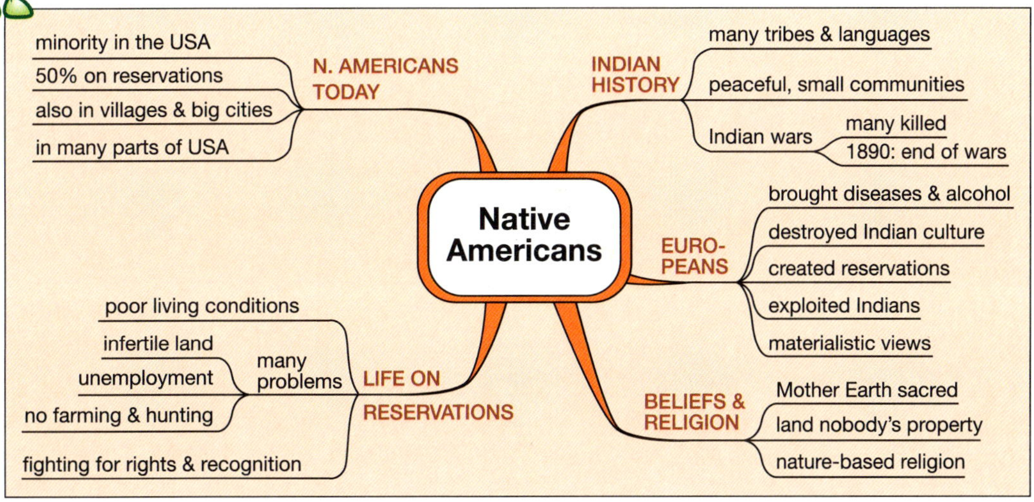

- With a mind map you may decide for yourself which main point you want to begin with to write a well structured text.

Planning the text by a topic outline

- A topic outline is a further method of arranging notes in an appropriate order. It can be written in words or in sentences.

Example: Native Americans (topic outline)

1. INDIAN HISTORY: ← Introduction
   - Live in peaceful communities ↓ Main part
   - Different tribes and languages
   - Indian wars, ended 1890
2. BELIEFS AND RELIGION
   - Mother Earth sacred
   - land nobody's property
   - nature-based religion

   Use a new paragraph for each main idea
3. EUROPEANS
   - brought diseases and alcohol
   - destroyed Indian culture
   - created reservations
   - exploited Indians
   - materialistic views
4. NATIVE INDIANS TODAY
   - minority
   - 50% on reservations
   - also in villages and big cities
   - in many parts of the USA
5. LIFE ON RESERVATIONS
   - poor living conditions
   - infertile land, unemployment, no farming and hunting
   - fighting for rights and recognition ← Conclusion

c) Writing a draft

While writing the draft

- Use A4-sheets of paper and leave a wide margin on the right side for corrections or additional ideas.
- Use your notes and plan as guidelines while writing.
- Try to catch your reader's attention with a lively opening.
- Arrange your text in paragraphs. (→ Writing a paragraph, pp. 45–46)

- Remember that a well structured text usually consists of three parts: Introduction, main part with its topical paragraphs, and conclusion. Each paragraph should be about one idea.
- Finish your text with a strong argument.

d) Revising the text

After writing the draft

Checking content and structure

- Check the content of your text and your paragraphing:
  - Have you left out any important ideas?
  - Are there any "weak" expressions and sentences that should be improved?
  - Is the logical development and clarity of your ideas all right?
  - Do you have to re-arrange paragraphs?
  - Have you used suitable connectives (→ pp. 121–122) to link your sentences and paragraphs?
  - Have you left enough space to separate the single paragraphs?

Checking language

- Finally read your text through carefully again and correct spelling and language errors.

e) Fair copy

- If, after your corrections your text does not look clean or is difficult to read, it is advisable to write a fair copy.
- Leave a margin in exam papers or in papers you have to hand in.
- Write clearly or type the text.
- Do not forget to proofread and correct your fair copy.

Writing a paragraph

A **paragraph** consists of a **group of sentences about one topic**. It begins with a topic sentence, which explains what the text is about. In a well structured paragraph a point is developed logically and, whenever possible, supported by facts and/or by examples. Ideas are put into coherent sentences which are linked up by **connectives**. Connectives are used within a sentence, from sentence to sentence, from paragraph to paragraph and when summing up ideas.

Connectives include:
- conjunctions: e.g. *and*, *although*, *so that*
- sequencers: e.g. *first of all*, *next*, *consequently*
- phrasal linkers: e.g. *as a result*, *in fact*, *all in all*

(→ Connectives, pp. 121–122)

A paragraph may look like this:

One topic only →	**Fateful diseases**	Connectives:
Topic sentence at → the beginning Ideas in a ↓ logical order	When the whites arrived on the North American continent, they brought manufactured goods that the Indians wanted and new fateful diseases that they did not. Certain of the new diseases proved particularly harmful to Indians because they did not have the immunity that the whites had developed through centuries of exposure. Above all contagious diseases, such as smallpox, venereal infections, and the rest, had disastrous effects on native society. Consequently all the Indian tribes were decimated by epidemics. In 1616-1617 a terrible epidemic swept over New England, killing many Indians, just a few years before the Pilgrims landed at Plymouth.	← in a sentence ← from sentence to sentence

And this is the structure of a longer text:

Introduction	Introductory paragraph	← Introduce the topic of your text in a few sentences and try to stimulate the reader's interest.
Main part Paragraphs ↓	1st main point Supporting point(s)	↓ Develop the topic and your points clearly in the following paragraphs. Remember: Each paragraph is about one main idea only. Link up paragraphs by connectives.
	2nd main point Supporting point(s)	
	3rd main point Supporting point(s)	
	etc.	
Conclusion	Concluding paragraph	← Sum up your results and finish with a general or personal statement.

How to quote

Quotations are words, phrases or sentences taken from other pieces of writing. They are used to support and prove what you say or write. There are two ways of quoting: In **direct quotations** the exact words of a text are repeated and put between quotation marks/inverted commas. In **indirect or reported quotations** the sense of a text you refer to is cited without quotation marks. In either case, references to the page(s) and the line number(s) of the source must be given. But for short texts, such as class tasks, line numbers will do. Longer passages of quoted material are set off from the left margin by further space.

Guidelines for quoted material

- When writing a paper, use a quote card for the material you borrow from different sources.
- Also jot down the bibliographical information of the source on that card.
- Remember that exact bibliographical data will help the reader to locate your source.
- A shortened bibliographical reference on the card will do, if you use the same source again.
- You may use the bottom of the card for short remarks.

Quote card

Bendelow, Paul: The man who likes the middle distance – Oliver Sacks. In: Lufthansa Bordbuch 2/96, pp. 38–41. Köln: Deutsche Lufthansa AG, 1996. ← exact source

pp. 39–40: ← page reference

"Since its publication in 1973, the book ['The man who mistook his wife for a hat'] has inspired radio and television documentaries, stage dramatisations including Harold Pinter's [...] play 'A Kind of Alaska', as well as the feature film 'Awakening' starring Robert de Niro as one of the patients and Robin Williams as the doctor based on Sacks himself." ← quotation

use quote for ch. 2

Rules for quotations

Oliver Sacks is a well known American Professor of Neurology who became famous all over the USA, when in 1995 his bestselling book 'An Anthropologist on Mars', a case history of neurologically damaged persons, was published.	← Single quotation marks are used to set off a title, a name, etc. within a quotation.
"Perhaps it is because of the film 'Awakenings' that there is something familiar about Oliver Sacks when you meet him in person. There is the big physical presence [...] of a well-fed bear, which Williams managed to project. But there is also the natural reserve of an intensively private person [and successful neurologist]." (Bendelow 1996, p. 40, ll. 5ff.)	← Quotation marks are used to indicate the repetition of someone's exact words. ← Square brackets and dots show that something of the original text has been left out. ← Square brackets are used to show that something has been added. ← Short form for the bibliographical data. If you refer to one page, write p. 38, for two pages use pp. 38–39, for more pages use pp. 38–41. When quoting lines, use l. 5 for one line, ll. 5f. for two lines and ll. 5ff. for more lines.
Sacks thought that his patients' experiences would be enormously reduced or distorted if they were published in a conventional medical periodical. (Cf. Bendelow 1996, p. 40, ll. 70ff.)	← Cf. (for compare) means that you have borrowed ideas from a text but not the exact words.

Listing books and articles (bibliography)

- At the end of your paper list the authors of the books and articles you consulted in alphabetical order, surname first.
- When quoting books, bibliographical data are usually arranged in the following order:

Quoting books

Author's or editor's name	Hinz, Klaus (Ed.) [Ed. short for editor]
Title of the book	Power Pack English. Skills and strategies for advanced learners.
Place of publication	Paderborn
Name of publishers	Schöningh Verlag im Westermann Schulbuchverlag
Year of publication	2003

Hinz, Klaus (Ed.): Power Pack English. Skills and strategies for advanced learners. Paderborn: Schöningh Verlag im Westermann Schulbuchverlag, 2003.

- When quoting articles, information is usually arranged like this:

Quoting articles

Author's name	Nattinger, John
Title of the article	Current trends in vocabulary studies
Author(s) of source	Carter, Ron and MacCarthy, Martin
Title of source	Vocabulary and language teaching
Place of publication	Harlow
Name of publishers	Longman Group Ltd
Year of publication	1988
Page numbers of article	195-209
Page number(s) used	207-209

Nattinger, John: Current trends in vocabulary studies. In: Carter, Ron and MacCarthy, Martin: Vocabulary and language teaching. Harlow: Longman Group Ltd, 1988, pp. 195–209; pp. 207–209.

How to produce different texts

Content questions

Answering **content questions** is the usual way of working on a text at home or in exams. The tasks following a literary or non-literary text can be divided into two groups, a) global and detailed comprehension questions and b) questions aiming at the composition, intention or effect of a text.

Comprehension – orientation

- You often have to answer comprehension questions in order to show whether you have understood the overall meaning and the details of a text before you advance to more complex questions.

Comprehension questions

- Questions of this type may read like this:
  - What is the text (passage) about?
  - What are the main ideas of the text?
  - What happens before/after he/she …?
  - Why does he …?
  - When do they …?

Analysis

- In answers to more demanding tasks you have to point out the deeper meaning of a text and you may need to analyse its structure and style.

Text analysis tasks

- Examples:
  - What kind of a man is …? Try to characterise him.
  - Examine how the ideas have been structured.
  - What is the point of view?
  - Find examples for the use of language and discuss their function.
  - Discuss how content and form go together.

Before writing

Reading and pre-writing activities

- Read the whole text right through to get its general sense. (→ Skimming, p. 12)
- Read the questions and make sure you understand exactly what they require of you.
- Read the text again guided by the content questions.
  Look up only words that you think are absolutely necessary to understand the text.

- Underline or mark those parts of the text that contain the information you need for your answers. Use a different colour for each question.
- Make notes and put them in a proper order. Use a grid if you want to. (→ p. 42)

While writing

Writing the draft

- Write a draft for each question along your notes.
- Answer each question fully, but do not repeat yourself.
- Use your own words and do not copy the original.
- If you decide to quote from the text put the words or sentence(s) in inverted commas and give the reference for the quote: page and line/s. (→ How to quote, pp. 47–49)

After writing

Text check

- Check your answers for language mistakes and correct them.
- If necessary, write a fair copy, especially for exam papers or papers you have to hand in. The examiner must be able to read your text without difficulty.

Example

Answer the following questions related to the short short story 'The ship' applying the foregoing writing technique.

1. What are the boy's experiences during the boat trip? (Comprehension/orientation)

   (This task asks you to describe what the boy sees and what his emotions are or may be like during the boat trip.)

2. How does the author manage to connect the boy's different impressions? (Analysis)

   (This task asks you to describe what stylistic means the author uses to make his story a unit, i.e. you need to work out the effect of the language.)

Joseph Bruchac ◆ The ship

I was a small boy. We were on board a steamship on a resort lake. As we went by the shore the captain would announce to the passengers details about the cottages on the banks.
"This is the estate," squawked the loudspeaker, "of the owner of the Algonquin Motor Lodge." A hugely windowed mansion with great pillars.
From the docks and the steps of boathouses people waved as we passed.
"This is the summer home of the President of the Albany Savings Bank."
I lifted my small arm and waved back.

"This is the summer home of …"

"You notice they don't tell where the poor people live," said a man wearing a worn blue shirt to the woman and child behind him. I noticed the woman's clothing was out of date and uncomfortable looking. I noticed the woman's hair was thinning and her face seemed to be worn thin like sandstone by wind. Then I noticed she was my mother.

I kept waving at the people on beaches and on floats, in boats and in the water. Then a little girl went by in a huge power boat driven by a man whom I knew must be her father. I waved … but she didn't wave back.

I looked up at my mother. "Little girl didn't wave."

"She didn't see you."

"But I wave to her. Why can't she …" My mother interrupted my words with a weary wave of her hand.

"Look around you!" she said.

I looked. The boat was full of mothers and children. They leaned over rails and dangled through portholes. All around were children my age, younger, older, in varying degrees of happiness and sorrow, good clothing and bad, clean faces and dirty. And each of them was waving, thinking the returned wave from the shore was for themselves alone.

Solution

Joseph Bruchac ◆ The ship

________ = question 1

marking = question 2

(parallelism)

I was a small boy. We were on board a steamship on a resort lake. As we went by the shore the captain would announce to the passengers details about the cottages on the banks.

"This is the estate," squawked the loudspeaker, "of the owner of the Algonquin Motor Lodge." A hugely windowed mansion with great pillars.

From the docks and the steps of boathouses people waved as we passed.

"This is the summer home of the President of the Albany Savings Bank."

I lifted my small arm and waved back.

"This is the summer home of …"

(repetition) ↓

"You notice they don't tell where the poor people live," said a man wearing a worn blue shirt to the woman and child behind him. I noticed the woman's clothing was out of date and uncomfortable looking. I noticed the woman's hair was thinning and her face seemed to be worn thin like sandstone by wind. Then I noticed she was my mother.

I kept waving at the people on beaches and on floats, in boats and in the water. Then a little girl went by in a huge power boat driven by a man whom I knew must be her father. I waved … but she didn't wave back.

I looked up at my mother. "Little girl didn't wave."

"She didn't see you."

"But I wave to her. Why can't she …" My mother interrupted my words with a weary wave of her hand.

"Look around you!" she said.

I looked. The boat was full of mothers and children. They leaned over rails and dangled through portholes. All around were children my age, younger, older, in varying degrees of happiness and sorrow, good clothing and bad, clean faces and dirty. And each of them was waving, thinking the returned wave from the shore was for themselves alone.

Question 1: What are the boy's experiences during the boat trip?

- The information needed to answer the question has been underlined in the text on p. 52. Collecting ideas:

what the boy sees:	what he feels:
• rich people's estates and summer homes • power boat (of rich people) • poorly clothed parents • girl in a power boat not returning his waving • steamship full of people (mixed group) • waving people	• not all people have the same status in life • not everybody pays attention to him • he feels ignored

- Ordering ideas:
  1. Not all people have the same status in life:
     - rich people's estates and summer homes
     - poorly clothed parents
     - mixed group of people in another boat
  2. He is just an individual out of a large number of people:
     - the girl in a power boat is not returning his waving

Answer

A small boy is on board a steamship on a resort lake. When the ship goes along the shore quite a few people standing there wave to the passengers and the boy waves back. ←**Introduction**

During the boat trip, he has two main experiences, first that not all people have the same status in life though his emotions are not really described by the author. The summer homes of rich people along the shore (ll. 4ff.) are quite a contrast to his poorly clothed parents (ll. 12ff.). The same is true of a mixed group of people in another boat: children "in good clothing and bad, clean faces and dirty" (ll. 26f.). ↓**Main part**

The second experience is the realization that he as an individual is just one out of a large number of fellow human beings. A girl passing by in a power boat ignores him and does not return his waving. His disappointment is great and the boy expresses it in his language: "Little girl didn't wave." – "But I wave to her." (ll. 19f.).

Disappointments are part of the process of growing up. ←**Conclusion**

Question 2: How does the author manage to connect the boy's different impressions?

- The stylistic devices the author uses to achieve his purpose have been marked in the text on p. 52. Notes:

> Stylistic devices:
>
> Parallelism:
> This is the … (ll. 4ff., yellow marking)
>
> Repetition:
> Notice … (ll. 11ff., blue marking)
> Wave … (ll. 16ff., green marking)
> Look … (ll. 19ff., pink marking)

Answer

Introduction → The language of the short story seems to be rather simple at first sight.
Main part ↓ But it is rhythmical and structured. The author uses several stylistic devices to make his story a unit, actually two units. These include parallelism and repetition. Right at the beginning, the sentence "This is the …" (ll. 4, 8, 10) establishes parallelism and creates a unit.
By repeating several verbs again and again ("notice": four times, ll. 11ff., "wave": six times, ll. 16ff., "look": three times, ll. 19ff.) the author connects the boy's impressions naturally and clearly and creates another unit.
Conclusion → Altogether the text gives the impression of a compact whole.

… And now it's your turn

George Orwell ◆ Serious sport is war minus the shooting (→ pp. 26–27)

Tasks:

1. What does Orwell mean when he says "Serious sport is war minus the shooting"? Collect ideas, order them and write the answer.
2. Try to determine the structure of the text. Put down headings for each paragraph in the margin and use them as an outline.

Summary

A **summary** is a shortened version of a longer text in your own words without personal opinions or an interpretation. It contains the most important information of the original text a reader or listener should know to get an idea of what it is about.

Before writing

- Read the text carefully and underline important key words and key phrases. You can also note down headings for the different paragraphs in the margin.
- Take notes of the important facts and ideas.
- Leave out information that is not essential, such as examples, detailed descriptions, statistics, etc.
- Make a topic outline (→ p. 44) or use a grid (→ p. 42) to order your material.

While writing

- Start with a sentence naming the writer and story title and stating its main idea.
- Write the summary using your notes as guidance.
- Use your own words as far as possible and do not copy sentences from the text.
- Do not add your own opinion or interpretation.
- Do not quote from the text but use your own language as much as possible.
- If necessary, change direct speech into reported speech.
- For summarising fictional texts use the present simple.

After writing

- Re-read your summary and check if you have followed the rules above.
- Have you covered all the essential points?
- Is your summary clear enough for somebody who does not know the original text?
- Have you used connectives (→ p. 121) to link your sentences?
- Have you checked your text for mistakes and correctness?

Example

Dennis Kurumada ◆ Just along for the ride (→ pp. 30–32)

Solution

- The following outline and the notes show the chronological development of the story and can be used for writing the summary.

Outline		Lines	Notes for the summary
Five friends driving around in a car.	(1)	1ff.	Dick steers the car, just got his licence, boys feel bored, need something to do.
Plan to knock somebody down.	(2)	13ff.	Plan: swing car door open and knock someone down, four boys agree, narrator disapproves.
They realise their plan, boy hit too hard, dash off afterwards.	(3)	25ff.	Car almost out of control, young person knocked down, narrator recognises him, it is his friend Ken Benjamin, he wants Dick to stop, driver dashes off, afraid of discovery and arrest.
Narrator is frightened and has a bad conscience.	(4)	68ff.	Dick takes friends home at midnight, narrator afraid to listen to the news, drives around, shocked and frightened, feels responsible, too.
Narrator's friends arrive at his home.	(5)	80ff.	Dick: Ken not hurt badly, wants the others to keep things secret, narrator gets furious, decides to drive to the Benjamins' house.

Answer

Introduction: → title, author, summarising sentence

The short story "Just along for the ride" was written by an American author named Dennis Kurumada. It is about a group of boys who aimlessly drive round town and carry out a vicious plan.

(1) driving around
(2) plan to knock someone down

In the exposition the author presents the two main characters: the unnamed narrator and Dick, who is driving his friends in his car. As the five boys are feeling bored and looking for some excitement, one of them suggests knocking someone down by opening the car door when passing him. All of them agree with the exception of the narrator who rejects the idea as dangerous and stupid.

(3) plan goes wrong

When, after some time, they spot a young male person, they put the plan into action. But unexpectedly he is hit too hard, thrown into the air and he rolls over the roof. Immediately the narrator tries to make Dick stop the car because he has recognised the boy, his friend Ken Benjamin. But the driver dashes off as quickly as possible in order not to be arrested for manslaughter.

(4) narrator feels responsible

(5) narrator's friends arrive at his home

Then Dick takes the boys back to their homes. At night the narrator drives around in his own car. He feels responsible, is shocked and does not know what to do. However, he feels that he is guilty, too. When he returns home, his friends are already waiting for him and they inform him that Ken has not been hurt seriously. When Dick wants the boys to keep the incident secret, the narrator gets furious and drives to the Benjamins' house. With this the story ends.

... And now it's your turn

Write a summary of the following article.

- Read the text carefully.
- Then gather notes on a separate sheet of paper.

Violence and vandalism in American schools

The fact is simple but stark[1]: vandalism and violence have become one of the foremost problems of the nation's schools. It is a problem that is elusive[2]; a costly problem that can strike without warning; a problem that involves fear of physical harm and emotional public demands for safer schools, and worst of all a problem that so far defies[3] solution.
Certainly vandalism and violence, to some degree, have been problems in schools at least since the uprisings in the nation's colleges and universities in the mid-1960s, but widespread awareness of their vast extent and pervasiveness[4] in elementary and secondary schools began to dawn with the coming of the 1970s.
In some big areas school administrators attest to extreme concern due to three factors: gang activity, the prevalence[5] of drugs, and the number of weapons finding their way onto school campuses, many times "carried for protection".
A senator from Indiana reported that in his state a ring was found operating in a junior high school which extorted[6] money from children. A committee of the New York State Legislative revealed that in some New York high schools students ran narcotics, firearms and prostitution rings. In explaining the impact of violence and vandalism on education, the senator said that the primary concern in many modern American schools is no longer education but preservation.
As shown by the Special Support Survey, almost everything in, on, near, part of, or belonging to a school, its staff or its students may be vandalized. The building itself is the most frequent target[7], particularly the windows. [...]

[1] **stark** here: shocking – [2] **elusive** difficult to describe or understand – [3] **the problem defies solution** no answer has been found yet – [4] **pervasiveness** of widespread nature – [5] **prevalence** state of being very common – [6] **to extort** to force sb. to give you money by threats of violence – [7] **target** here: victim

Giving opinions

Giving opinions is a type of comment in which you express your personal views and give reasons how you see and evaluate a given problem. This text form is based on a response to a controversial idea, suggestion, criticism, etc. It usually consists of these parts: a) presenting the topic, b) giving opinions, c) supporting opinions by facts, examples, personal experience, etc., d) conclusion.

Before writing

- Brainstorm on the topic and gather ideas, facts, examples, etc. to support your opinion and arguments. (→ Argumentative texts, p. 23)
- If your task is text-related, check the text for ideas you can make use of.
- Make notes for your response to the problem and develop an opinion.
- Think about facts and examples you want to use to underpin or contradict the controversial subject in question and note them down.
- Order and number your points.

While writing

- Begin with an introduction that presents the problem or topic you want to discuss.
- State your position on the problem.
- Develop your point of view while using the notes you have made.
- Organise your response in paragraphs. Use one paragraph for each topic.
- Finally sum up your opinion and point out the consequences of your position in a general statement.

After writing

- Check your text for the logical development of ideas.
- Make sure you have expressed your position clearly enough by using convincing facts and examples.
- Proofread your text for language errors and correct them.

Example

In the following article a member of an animal activist group gives his opinion on “Animals in captivity”.

Animals in captivity

The concept of animal rights has come to play an important role in several areas of concern over human treatment of other animals. These areas range from the hunting and trapping of animals to obvious cases of mistreatment in factory farming where animals live in relatively small areas.

Animals in captivity have always been a controversial subject. Some feel that 'kidnapping' animals is dreadful and they should be free in their natural habitat, while others believe that having animals in captivity, for example in zoos, creates a better understanding of animals for the world.

According to 'The Humane Society of the United States' and similar organisations for the protection of our fellow creatures, keeping animals in captivity is immoral. All of them agree that for example whales physically suffer from the limited movement allowed in small artificial pools. They go through much social deprivation when removed from their families in the wild, and suffer shorter life spans than their counterparts in the wild.

Their movements are appallingly restricted to endless circlings in the pool. As a matter of fact behavioural studies on captive whales cannot be applied to wild whales because captivity forces these animals to behave unnaturally.

Animals in circuses is a further example of mistreatment. The image that many people have of the circus is of a spectacular and wondrous world full of colour, music, glitter, fun and excitement, where artists, lion tamers and clown perform amazing acts to delight the audience. But there is another side to the world of the circus: one that you are not supposed to notice.

Most people who go to see a circus with performing animals are totally unaware of the cruelty and suffering that lies behind this illusion of harmless fun.

When animals first arrive at the circus they must suffer abuse and humiliation. First they must be tamed and then trained and taught tricks. This is done with a combination of rewards and punishments and without a doubt many of the methods used to train the animals are terribly cruel, stressful and unnatural.

Some examples of the sorts of degrading and humiliating animal acts performed to an audience include bears that are made to ice skate, tigers that are made to ride on the backs of rhinos or balance in a begging position on large glittering balls, and elephants that are made to stand on their head or front legs.

"What has the elephant done, what crime has the elephant committed that it should be kept in chains?" Dr Paul Harris, a renowned elephant expert, asked.

Fortunately, there is a growing awareness and many people feel ashamed by the spectacle of once-proud animals being degraded and humiliated for our entertainment. Animals in this country deserve better protection and we want to see legislation that would ban circuses with performing animals.

← Headline presents topic

← **Introduction:** animal rights, mistreatment

↓ **Main part:**

- captivity a controversial subject
- keeping animals immoral, harmful, unnatural
- 1st example: whales
- supporting details
- 2nd example: circuses
- two sides of animal performances
- animals suffer abuse and humiliation
- supporting details

← **Conclusion:** growing awareness, people feel ashamed, appeal to the public and politicians

Solution

- If you want to give your opinion on this controversial subject, the notes in the following net diagram could serve as the basis.

Collecting information:

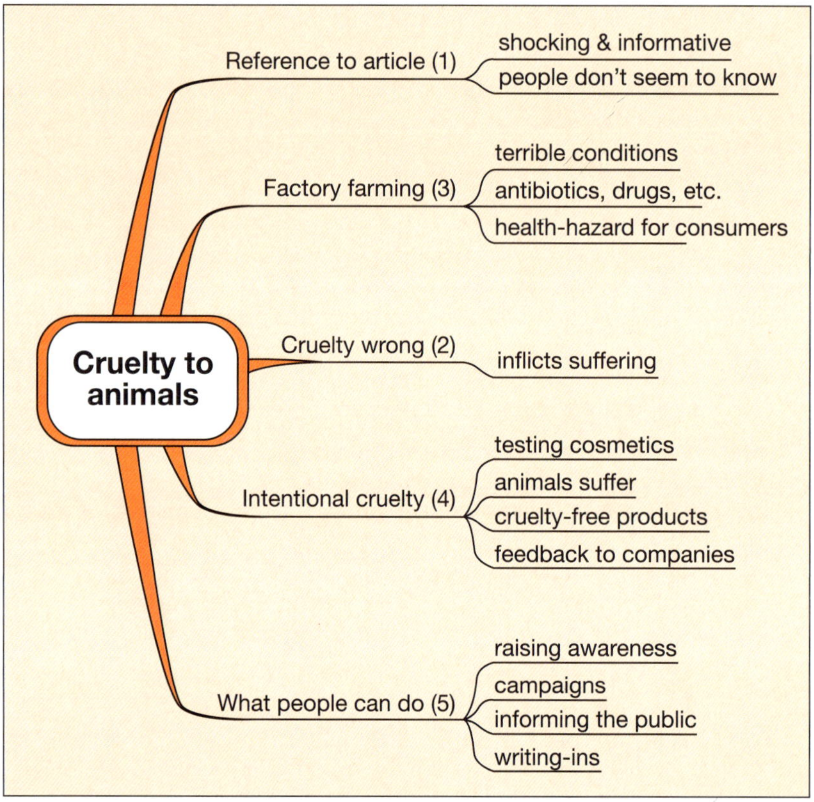

Answer

Introduction: → reference to topic in actual text (1)

The article "Animals in captivity" is informative and shocking at the same time. Many people do not seem to consider what animals have to suffer before being able to perform acts that are virtually against their nature, in circuses or in pools where dolphins and whales are restricted to a limited space.

Main part: ↓
- 1st subtopic: cruelty general concern (2)
- example: factory farming (3)

All animal cruelty is a general concern because it is wrong to inflict suffering on any living creature. A further example is factory farming, which is a method of raising large numbers of poultry or livestock in relatively small areas, under terrible conditions. The large concentration of animals in confinement makes it necessary to prevent epidemics. So growth stimulants, antibiotics and other drugs are added to feed or injected directly into the animals. This is an enormous health hazard to us, the consumers.

Intentional cruelty is a further concern, which is practised in the laboratories of cosmetic companies where cosmetic products and ingredients are tested on animals. It should be generally accepted that the production of new cosmetics should not cause animal suffering. Consumers can contribute to changing animals' shocking living conditions by asking for 'cruelty free' cosmetics in the shops. The feedback the companies will surely get may convince them that it is reasonable to stop animal testing.

- 2nd subtopic: intentional cruelty (4)
- example: testing cosmetics on animals

All people to whom animal suffering is a concern should do something to help our suffering fellow creatures by raising people's awareness. But awareness needs organisation, such as campaigns and must be accompanied by leaflets, fact sheets, writing-in actions to the media and politicians.

← **Conclusion:** ways to raise public awareness (5)

... And now it's your turn

Fox-hunting – for and against (→ pp. 24–25)

Read the interview and give your opinion on sport of that nature.

Text evaluation

Evaluating a text is a task often set in class. It comprises tasks such as
- giving comments on a whole text or part of it,
- expressing opinions on the topic of the text or the way the author deals with it,
- integrating the topic or its theses into a wider context, etc.

Before writing

Reading and collecting information

- Before you work on the task, make sure that you have completely understood the text.
  In class, simple comprehension questions have to be answered first before you are asked to evaluate a text.
- Read the task and make sure you have completely understood it.
- Read the text again guided by the task.
- Underline or mark those parts of the text that contain the information you need for your answer.
- Make notes and then put them in a proper order. It may be useful to enter them in a grid. (→ p. 42)

While writing

Writing the draft

- Write a draft along your notes.
- If you decide to quote from the text put the words or sentence(s) in inverted commas and give the reference for the quote: page and line/s. (→ How to quote, pp. 47–49)

After writing

- Check your text for language mistakes and correct them.
- If necessary, write a fair copy, especially for exam papers or papers you have to hand in. The examiner must be able to read your text without difficulty.

Example

Joseph Bruchac ◆ The ship (→ pp. 51–52)

Task: On the basis of what you know about the short short story 'The ship' (cf. pp. 53f.), enlarge on the main theme and say how it can be integrated into a wider context.

(It is absolutely necessary that you have completely understood the story and its structure and know what the boy has experienced during the boat trip. Your task is to work on the problem, write about the main theme in detail and put it in a wider context, i.e. what you have learnt in your lessons or what you know about it from experience.)

Solution

- Notes:

  - *point of view: first-person narrator*
  - *main theme:*
    contrast between the rich and the poor
  - *rich people:*
    owners of summer homes
  - *poor people:*
    people on holiday
  - *wider context:*
    other story about growing up

Answer

Introduction → The short short story 'The ship' is written from a first-person point of view and is about fundamental experiences we will all have had at some time in our lives.

Main part ↓ The most important experience is the realisation that not all people are equal. The wealthy owners of summer homes are contrasted with the poor holidaying people. The boy's family serves as an example of poverty against which the rich side of life is set off. The boy's parents probably belong to the working class, their clothes show that they are not well-off: "the woman's clothing [is] out of date and uncomfortable looking" (l. 12f.), and the man wears "a worn blue shirt" (l. 12). The differences between people's stations in life are also referred to in the description of the children on the other steamship: "... children in varying degrees of happiness and sorrow, good clothing and bad, clean faces and dirty." (ll. 26f.)

← **Conclusion**

The contrast between rich and poor is often thematised in other stories, for instance in ... [a few remarks on a story you have read]. The insight into this aspect of social reality is part of growing up.

... And now it's your turn

George Orwell ◆ Serious sport is war minus the shooting (→ pp. 26–27)

Task: Comment on the author's attitude toward sport.

(Collect and order ideas in a chart and write the text.)

Reporting events

Reports present accounts of recent or current events that can be checked. They provide objective information of facts in chronological order by answering the **five w-questions and h-question:** Who did what, when, where, why and how? Reports aim at informing readers to enable them to form their own opinion. In school tasks that require writing reports you will have to refer to factual and also to fictitious events or incidents in texts you have read. Well-known variants are news reports and news stories in newspapers. They often contain the writer's opinion and want to entertain. (→ Report, pp. 20-23)

Before writing

Collecting and ordering material

- Carefully consider what your report will be about.
- Collect the essential facts that answer the six questions: who?, what?, when?, where?, why? and how?
- Use a grid (→ p. 42) or a similar structural aid to order your notes.
- Make sure that your notes are complete and correct.
- If your report is based on fictitious events, e.g. in a short story or play, you may have to add further details such as surnames, place names, time spans, etc.

While writing

- Write your report using the six questions and your notes as a guide.
- Begin your report with a summarising sentence.
- Create a chronological order of events by using time words.
- If you write a longer report, divide it into paragraphs.
- Use the past tense for the reported facts.
- Use language that is objective in style and content.
- Apply a formal matter-of-fact style.
- Aim at achieving objectivity, precision, clarity and completeness.
- Use exact quotes, if necessary.

Time words
- Time adverbs: e.g. *at first*, *then*, *later*, *afterwards*, *finally* …
- Time adverbials: e.g. *a short time later*, *in the meantime*, *after about an hour* …
- Time clauses: e.g. *when* …, *as soon as* …, *while* …, *before* …, *after* …

After writing

- Re-read your report for factual correctness and clarity.
- Check if your language is clear enough and easy to understand.
- Proofread your report for language errors and correct them.
- If necessary, write a fair copy.

Example

Dennis Kurumada ◆ Just along for the ride (→ pp. 30–32)

As Denny had phoned the police about the incident, they wanted to see him for an interview and bring a written report.

Solution

- The following notes that answer the five w's and h-question serve as the basis for the report.
- Note: As this short story does not supply all the necessary information needed for a complete report, the missing facts have been added in blue type.

Collecting ideas:

Questions & details	Facts & additions (in blue)
Who (is involved)?	Dick Bakers (driver) Phil Murray (sitting in front) Reid Hawker (in the back) Steve Anderson (in the back) Denny White (narrator, in the back) Ken Benjamin (victim)
What (did they do)?	Hit and hurt a young person
When (did it happen)?	Last night, about 10 pm
Where (did it happen)?	In Woodland Road, near John's drugstore
Why (did it happen)?	Boredom, friends needed something to do
How (did it happen)?	Plan: open car door and knock someone down Accident: car swerved, hit victim who rolled over car roof

- For a detailed report more factual information is needed.
- As the necessary points appear in the story in chronological order, they do not need further arrangement.

Notes:

- four friends driving around
- last night, at about 10 pm
- Phil's plan to hit somebody
- Dick, Reid and Steve agreed
- looked around for a victim
- Denny's warning
- discovered young person
- boy stepped out into street
- car swerved
- victim hit by car
- Dick sped down road
- Denny asked driver to stop
- Dick refused
- Dick drove boys home at 0.30
- four friends returned at 2 am
- information: Ben not hurt seriously
- Dick: keep it secret

Answer

Report on the accident in Woodland Road on friday, 20.11.200..

Summarising sentence · When … · Who …

I was a passenger in the runaway car and want to give evidence in this eyewitness account. The accident, in which Ken Benjamin was hurt, happened at about 10 o'clock pm on 20.11.200..
At about 9.30 pm Dick Bakers, who had just got his driving licence, picked me up. My other friends were already in the car: Phil Murray was sitting next to Dick Bakers, who was driving, Reid Hawker, Steve Anderson and myself were seated in the back.

Why … · Where … · What … plan · Victim discovered · How … accident · Denny's friend

The five of us were bored and decided to drive around. When we were moving down Woodland Road towards John's drugstore, Phil Murray suggested that we should drive up to someone, open the car door and hit him. The others agreed to the plan. I warned them but they would not listen. When Phil Murray shouted that he had discovered a young person, Dick Bakers started moving his car from side to side. At that moment the boy stepped out into the street and the car began to swerve. The driver wanted to get the car back away from the boy but it was too late. He was hit and rolled over the roof. I recognised the victim. He was my friend Ken Benjamin. Although I told Dick to stop the car, he dashed away at a high speed.

Further information

Later Dick took us home. It must have been at about 0.30. At 2 am my friends returned. Dick informed me he had heard on the news that Ken Benjamin had not been hurt seriously and that we should all keep the incident secret.
As I could not accept that suggestion, I have reported the accident to the police.

Denny White

… And now it's your turn

Ernest Hemingway ◆ At two o'clock in the morning (→ p. 98)

Read the story and then write Drevitts' report for the Head of the Police Department.

Informal and formal letters

There are no fixed rules for **informal letters** as they are an individual matter. This also applies to fax messages and e-mails you send to members of the family and people you are familiar with. **Formal letters** are written to organisations or to people you do not know well or not at all. You may for example apply for a job, make a complaint, a request or write to the editor of a newspaper. In formal letters certain rules have to be observed, such as the layout, style, degree of politeness and the choice of language.

Before writing

Informal letters:

- As you usually refer to a letter you have received, mark the points you intend to respond to.
- Collect some more points you want to mention.
- Order your points and notes.

Formal letters:

- Carefully consider whom you are writing your letter to, why you are writing it, and what you want to say or to achieve.
- Note down the facts, points or ideas you may want to write about.
- Arrange your material in a logical order. Use a grid (→ p. 42) or a similar technique.

> **Letters** are usually divided into 3 parts: a) reason for writing
> b) the subject
> c) polite conclusion

While writing

- Write your letter along your ordered notes.
- In your introduction briefly say why you are writing.
- Take care that the style, language and layout of your letter is appropriate to the receiver and the purpose of writing.

> **Informal style:** It is used between people who feel comfortable and familiar with each other. It is characterised by the use of rather colloquial, sometimes even slangy language, short forms and uncomplicated sentence structures.
>
> **Formal style:** It is used e.g. when writing to organisations, institutions, etc. or people you do not know very well. It is characterised by the neutral use of language, careful choice of vocabulary, complex sentence structures and full forms. Formal style usually keeps a distance between writer and receiver.

After writing

- Make sure you have covered all the important points you wanted to write about.
- Re-read your letter for factual correctness and clarity.
- Make sure you have applied the proper layout, suitable language and degree of politeness.
- Check your letter for language errors and correct them.

Examples

1. Informal letter: An e-mail to a pen friend

Informal salutation →	Hi Luisa,
Text begins with capital letter → Informal tone ↓ and style of writing	Here I'm again. I've got great news for you. You are still looking for a job over here, aren't you? Our neighbours (rich) are looking for a German student to accompany them on their holiday to Cornwall. I have of course told them about you. They would like you to brush up their children's German. Their names: Sally, 12 and Richard, 13. They are nice and not very difficult – hopefully. They attend a Public School but don't seem to be very good at languages. The Evansons want you to write a few lines about yourself and your family soon. Interested? This is your great chance! Take it. Write to Ms Mary Evanson, 48 Stevenage Road, London SWE6 6NR.
Concluding phrase →	Good luck and ring me soon.
Familiar closing phrase →	Lots of love,
Typed signature (e-mail) →	Julia

Informal conclusions:

- Best wishes
- All the best
- With kind(est) regards
- Best regards
- Love
- Lots of love

Formal conclusions:

- Yours faithfully
  (If you do not know the name of the person you are writing to.)
- Yours sincerely
  (If you know the name of the person you are writing to.)

2. Formal letter: Luisa's letter of application

- The following notes may be the basis for the letter. The numbers in brackets refer to the order of points.

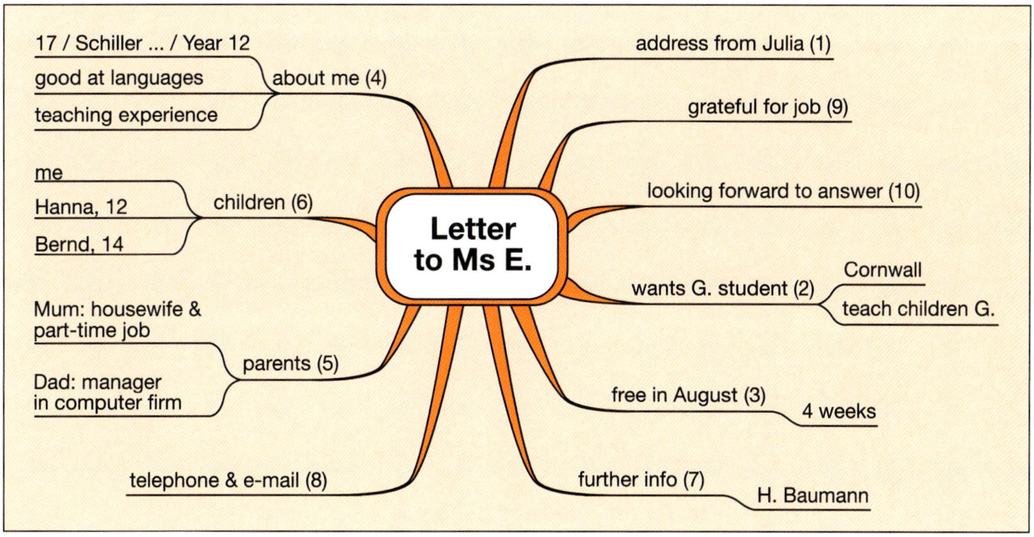

Letter

Writer's address in top right corner, ← without name

Castelleweg 5
D- 32051 Herford
0 52 21-12 34 56 ← Phone number
L.Grosse@maxweb.de. ← E-mail address

12 April 200_ ← Date below the address

Ms Mary Evanson
48 Stevenage Road
London SWE6 6NR
England

← Receiver's name and address on the left-hand side

Dear Ms Evanson, ← Salutation

↓ Body of letter in paragraphs
← Introduction: (1) reason for writing

I received your name and address from my English pen friend Julia Raymond who lives in your street. She informed me that you are looking for a German student to accompany your family on a holiday trip to Cornwall in August this year to offer your two children the possibility to practise and improve their German. (2)
As August is a school holiday month here in Germany, I could stay with you for four weeks. (3)
I am 17 years old and in Year 12 at the local Schiller Grammar School. Languages are my favourite subjects. I am already experienced in giving private lessons to pupils to help them solve their language problems. (4)
We are a family of five. My mother is a housewife and works as a part- (5)

time secretary. My father is a manager in a computer firm. I have got a
(6) sister (12) and brother (14) who also attend the Schiller Grammar School.
If you want further information about me, my English teacher has
(7) agreed to write to you. His name and address are: Herr Harald Baumann, Schiller Gymnasium, Schiller Straße 37, D-32054 Herford.
(8) Besides writing a letter you can also contact me by e-mail or by telephone.
(9) I would be very grateful if you would consider me for the position.
(10) I am looking forward to hearing from you soon.

Closing phrase → Yours sincerely

Writer's signature → Luisa Grosse

Writer's full name → (Luisa Grosse)

... And now it's your turn

Write Ms Evanson's letter of acceptance to Luisa.

Letter to the editor

A **letter to the editor** belongs to the group of formal letters and requires the use of the same rules for the layout, style, etc. It is a variant of the text form "Giving opinions" (→ pp. 58–61).
People often write to a newspaper if they want to express their views on a controversial problem previously discussed in a particular paper or in other media, usually with the intention of having the letter published. In school you may be asked to write a letter to the editor after reading a news article, another reader's letter, after watching the TV news or discussing a point of general interest. Address the receiver as "Madam or Sir", not as "Dear ...", and conclude with your full name and place of residence. Generally, "Yours faithfully" is not used to finish off.

Before writing

- Read through the text, watch a videotaped news report, etc. you want to react to in your letter and note down the important facts and points.
- Brainstorm further ideas you may want to use and arrange them in a logical order.

While writing

- In your first sentence mention the article, the general problem, etc. you want to respond to.

- Write your letter along your ordered notes.
- Back up your arguments with evidence and examples whenever possible.
- Take care that the layout and style of your letter is appropriate for your writing purpose.
- Decide how to conclude. (Call for action? Emotive/critical/ironical/etc. statement? A question to leave the reader thinking?)
- Keep in mind that a newspaper will not allow you too much space; therefore draft a letter of about 200 words.
- As the editorial staff decides whether to publish your letter or not, it is advisable to hand in a clean and readable copy.

After writing

- Make sure you have covered all the important points.
- Re-read your letter for factual correctness and clarity.
- Check your letter for language errors and correct them.

Example

This article appeared in a national newspaper. Write a response to the editor.

Doctors call for total ban on smoking in public

Sarah Boseley, health editor

Doctors yesterday called for a total ban on smoking in public places such as offices, factories, pubs and restaurants, arguing that second-hand cigarette smoke kills at least 1,000 people a year and puts 17,000 small children in hospital.

A hard-hitting report from the British Medical Association spelling out[1] the hidden dangers of inhaling other people's tobacco smoke was warmly welcomed by the campaigning[2] group Action on Smoking and Health. […]

The BMA[3] says there is general acceptance that passive smoking is bad for health, but that voluntary agreements to restrict smoking in offices and restaurants do not offer enough protection. According to the report, 3 million workers are regularly exposed to second-hand smoke. […]

Vivienne Nathanson, head of ethics at the BMA, said every other country in Europe had some legislation on passive smoking and it was time Britain caught up.

"There is no doubt there has been a shift in public mood," she said. "People are beginning to recognise that the reason why we see so many children getting asthma and missing school has a relation to their exposure to tobacco smoke." […]

Passive smoking cannot only cause lung cancer, increase the risk of stroke[4] and worsen asthma, but can also cause coronary[5] heart disease. […]

[1] **to spell sth. out** to explain something clearly and in detail – [2] **to campaign** to take part in a series of actions intended to achieve a particular result – [3] **BMA** British Medical Association – [4] **stroke** *Schlaganfall* – [5] **coronary** concerning the heart

Solution

- The following notes serve as the basis for the letter. The numbers refer to the order of points.

• anti-smoking campaigns	(5)
• why tolerate smokers?	(7)
• smokers affect health of children	(10)
• people know health risks (media)	(3)
• non-smokers to fight back	(11)
• no new facts in article	(2)
• smokers must be stopped	(12)
• BMA: information and opinions	(4)
• feeling maltreated	(1)
• appeal to reason does not work	(6)
• smokers don't care, they continue	(8)
• smoking in spite of warnings	(9)

The letter

Formal salutation → Madam or Sir,

Introduction: → reason for writing
I read your Nov. 6 article "Doctors call for total ban on smoking in public" and I feel compelled to protest.

Body of letter ↓ in paragraphs
(1) I am a non-smoker who is constantly maltreated by those people who think that they can light up whenever and wherever they are.
(2) What facts does the article contain that the public has not known already?
(3) For years people in Britain have been watching and reading in the media that there is no doubt that smoking is dangerous and damages the health. This is also true of passive smoking.
(4) The BMA just lists up pieces of information and opinions. But what we urgently need in this country are more calls for more
(5) campaigns against smoking in public places.
(6) I personally believe that an appeal to reason does not work. Smokers just do not care about their anti-social behaviour. Can anybody tell me why I
(7) should tolerate passive smoking? Large numbers of people, including a
(8) growing proportion of youngsters, continue to smoke in spite of all warn-
(9) ings. By doing so they are thoughtlessly affecting the health of those around
(10) them, among them innocent children who cannot protect themselves.
If smokers are foolish enough to continue their dangerous habit, it is high
(11) time that non-smokers fought back. The question can no longer be whether
(12) smoking should be banned in public places – it must be banned. The sooner the better!

Writer's signature and place of residence →
Elizabeth Dawson
Brighton

Writer's typed name → (Elizabeth Dawson)

... And now it's your turn

Write a letter to the editor: "What can be done to protect teenagers from the dangers of smoking?"

Characterisation

The people in fictional texts, such as short stories, plays or novels, are called characters. They are presented through their main features, e.g. their behaviour, appearance, attitudes and language, their thoughts and actions, and also by description. When writing a **characterisation** it is important to recognise and explain how an author presents her/his characters and what they are like.

Before writing

- Read the text carefully and mark all the important points that help you describe the character(s):
  - name and position (what job they do)
  - social background (where and how they live, their family and education)
  - physical/outward appearance (what they look like)
  - language (choice of words, the way they talk)
  - thoughts (what they think)
  - aspects of character (their attitudes, feelings, ideas, temperament)
  - development of character (change of attitudes)
  - actions (what they do)
  - interaction (the way they behave towards others)
  - hearsay (what other people think or say about them)

> In fictional texts people can be characterised in two ways:
>
> - **Direct characterisation:**
>
> The reader is informed about a character in a story, a drama, etc. who makes comments or judgments.
>
> - **Indirect characterisation:**
>
> The reader draws his own conclusions about a character through his/her behaviour, opinions, use of language and his/her way of dealing with problems or other people.

- Decide on how to organise your findings:
  - You could use the order as listed up in the preceding point.
  - You may underline important evidence while reading the text and number it in the margin later.
  - You can also arrange it in a grid (→ p. 42) or mind map (→ p. 43).

While writing

- Start with a short introduction and present the setting, situation, and the character(s).
- Write the characterisation in a coherent text using your numbered notes.
- Arrange your text into paragraphs. Each one should deal with one important feature only.
- Point out how the different features of a character are connected with each other.
- Present the evidence from the text and comment on it.
- Remember to put quotes between quotation marks and put the line number(s) in round brackets. (→ How to quote, pp. 47–49)
- Finally write a conclusion and sum up your findings.

After writing

- Check if you have followed the foregoing rules.
- Make sure that your characterisation includes all the important notes you have made.
- Have you supported your characterisation convincingly by referring to or quoting important evidence?
- Make sure that you have connected your results and sentences properly.
- Finally proofread your text and correct spelling and grammar mistakes.

Example

Task: Characterise Mr. Mumsford.

When you read the following story for the first time, ignore the markings in the text. They will be referred to in the next step.

Larry French ◆ Mr. Mumsford

Bibs, the janitor[1], had never killed a man before. He'd raised rabbits as a boy and killed one now and then for supper. A quick blow to the back of the neck, and it was done. He was not a particularly intelligent man and was not suffering from guilt or any philosophical questions about what he was going to do. He had come to the small southern school as a janitor twenty-seven years ago. On his first day at school, he had worn a pair of old bib overalls and thus earned the nickname of Bibs[2]. This was the reason he had come to kill the principal[3] who was working late in his office down the hall. Earlier in the evening, Bibs had gone into the equipment room and picked out the largest baseball bat he could find. He then went and hid in a space between the green metal lockers that lined the hallways. At a little past ten the principal walked out of his office, locked it, and started down the hall. Bibs stepped out in front of him.

"Say, Bibs," asked the principal. "What are you doing here this time of night?"

Beads[4] of sweat stood out on Bib's forehead, and he clenched[5] the bat with both hands. He was six feet tall, very black, and towered over the principal.

"I come to kill you," said Bibs.

"But why? What have I ever done to you?"

"Just what you called me is why!" said Bibs. "Nobody in this school, including you, has ever bothered to learn my real name. Onliest person knows my real name is that woman signs my check, and even she puts it in an envelope marked BIBS. The kids should learn my name in four years. Hell, I know more'n half of their names and where they live. This morning I stopped a couple of 'em and asked 'em did they know my real name, and they looked at me like I was crazy. That's why I come to kill you!"

The principal was a short man anyway, but now his shoulders slumped[6] even further, and he looked sad and confused.

"Well," he said. "Well, what is your name?"

"Ralph Mumsford," said Bibs.

"Mumsford's a strange name for a black man to have," said the principal. It's English, isn't it?"

"I don't know."

"You should look it up," said the principal. "You should go over to the school library and look it up. Say, lookee here, if I promise me and all my teachers call you by your real name from now on, will you not kill me?"

Bibs thought for a moment, seemed to waver[7], and then said, "Well, that seems fair. You do that, and I won't have to kill you."

The principal looked tired.

"You been working too many hours," said Bibs. "A Christian man ought to always eat the supper meal with his wife."

The principal sighed and said, "I do believe you're right, Mr. Mumsford. I do believe you have a point there." Then he turned and walked down the dark corridor toward the green exit sign leading out to the playground.

[1] **janitor** (AE) caretaker – [2] **bib** a cover worn by little children when eating to protect their clothes from getting dirty – [3] **principal** (AE) headmaster – [4] **bead** small drop of liquid – [5] **to clench** to hold firmly – [6] **to slump** to fall – [7] **to waver** to hesitate

Solution

Gathering and ordering information

The markings in the story have been arranged in the following way:

Name and job	Outward appearance	Social status and education	Reasons for the plan	Mental nature
– Bibs – Mr. Mumsford – janitor at southern school – for about 27 years	– very black – 6 feet tall – taller than principal	– minor job – dressed in old bib overall – not very intelligent – non-standard American English	– worried – bothered by nickname	– ambiguous – soft and gentle – aggressive – not suffering from guilt – not conscience-stricken – beads of sweat – gentle again – compassion

Characterisation

Introduction →

Bibs, whose real name is Ralph Mumsford, has been working as a janitor at a small southern school for about twenty-seven years. Now he seems to be dissatisfied with his situation and with the principal in particular.

Main part ↓
outward appearance

Ralph is a big person and coloured: "He was six feet tall, very black, and towered over the principal" (l. 16). On the first day at the school he was wearing a pair of bib overalls which is the reason why he is always called by the nickname Bibs. This worries him very much.

mental nature: ambiguous, gentle, aggressive, brutal

Although he has never shown any signs of an aggressive or brutal nature, not even against animals – when he killed a rabbit for a meal, he did it quickly (l. 2ff.) – he one day decides to kill the principal because he can no longer stand being referred to only by nickname. Surprisingly he is not "suffering from guilt" (l. 4) nor is he conscience-stricken by his horrible plan. But his feeling of uneasiness becomes obvious when "beads of sweat" (l. 15) appear on his forehead.

low education: language intelligence

Bibs often speaks non-standard English and uses incorrect grammatical structures. And he is not "a particularly intelligent man" (l. 3) either as he carries out his plan without thinking and rather hastily. Instead of taking the principal by surprise, he just walks up to him and says: "I come to kill you" (l. 17).

In the course of their conversation the principal manages to persuade Bibs to give up his plan. When he promises that from now on all the teachers will call him by his real name, Bibs first considers the promise, then he "seemed to waver" (l. 36) and at last accepts: "Well, that seems fair. You do that, and I won't have to kill you" (l. 36f.) Now his real good nature has re-appeared and he even shows compassion for the principal before they depart.

mental nature: gentle character re-appears, compassion

Conclusion →

In this short story the reader meets a simple character who has been refused his real name for a long time and who has recognised that he has not been taken seriously by being nicknamed all the time. Though he is a simple, uneducated person, he has been able to teach the principal of the school a thoughtful lesson.

... And now it's your turn

Dennis Kurumada ◆ Just along for the ride (→ pp. 30–32)

Write a characterisation of the narrator.

Continuation of a fictional text

The **continuation** of a fictional text is a creative task. But it is based on the text you are reading or have been reading in class. As your task refers to what happened before, a good knowledge of the actual text is required.

Before writing

- Read through the story carefully again.
- Make notes on the following points:
  - From what point of view is the story presented?
  - What atmosphere does the writer create?
  - How do the characters behave and react? What are their attitudes?
  - What conflict does the story deal with?
  - Is there tension between the characters?
  - What is their relationship towards each other?
  - Are there any clues or foreshadowing hints how the story might continue?
  - What kind of language, stylistic devices and sentence structure does the author use?
- Brainstorm and gather ideas about how the story might go on.
- Use a grid (→ p. 42), a note-taking chart (→ p. 42) or another structural aid to order your points.

Point of view: The perspective from which a story is presented. A story may be told by a first-person narrator, e.g. by one of the characters or by a third-person narrator who stands outside the story. The latter can be omniscient (unlimited point of view), or present the events, etc. through a character's eyes (limited point of view).
Atmosphere: The feeling or mood created by the writer through the description of characters, events, setting, situation, etc. to evoke emotions; it may be, for example, pleasant, mysterious or threatening.
Conflict: A problem the main characters in a drama, novel, etc. are involved in and that mostly leads to a clash. If a struggle takes place inside a character's mind, this is called internal conflict.
Suspense: It means an expectation aroused in the reader or audience about the future development of the plot, conflict and characters in a fictional text.
Tension: It is created when a drama or novel shifts between conflict situations and calmer passages or episodes in which tension eases off.

While writing

- Start writing your story along the lines of your ordered notes.
- Make sure that your continuation is plausible even if you decide to write a surprise ending.
- Try to stay close to the author's style and language.

After writing

- Make sure that there aren't any inconsistencies in your continuation of the actual text.
- Check if your text is close enough to the language of the original.
- Proofread your text for grammar and spelling mistakes.

Example

Larry French ◆ Mr. Mumsford (→ pp. 74–75)

Task: Continue the short story 'Mr. Mumsford'.

Solution

- The following points serve as the basis for the continuation. The numbers in brackets refer to the order of points.

- principal disappears (1)
- wants to let his wife know (6)
- remembers: "Name English?" (10)
- principal called him "Mr. Mumsford" (5)
- feeling of pride (4)
- advice to go to school library (11)
- cannot read well (13)
- teachers will call him "Mr. Mumsford" (7)
- principal's promise (8)
- name on envelope (9)
- locks and tries school doors (14)
- takes bat back (3)
- kids might wonder and giggle (12)
- bat still in his hand (2)
- walks home proudly (17)
- leaves school premises (16)
- lamp switched on (15)

Continuation

(1) Bibs watched the principal as he slowly crossed the playground until he
disappeared in the dark. It was only then that he became aware that he
(2) was still clenching the baseball bat with his right hand. Slowly he went
back to the equipment room at the end of the corridor and with a quick
(3) movement he flung it back to where it belonged. "Mr. Mumsford", it
echoed in his mind. He wasn't Bibs any longer. A feeling of pride was
(4) creeping up in him from his stomach. Once at home, he would immedia-
(5) tely tell his wife: "Principal called me by my real name. Called me twice
(6) Mr. Mumsford." And of course he would not forget to let her know that
(7) the other teachers would also call him by his real name from the next day
(8) on. The principal had promised it. And the envelope with his cheque in it
(9) would also read now "Mr. Ralph Mumsford".

Suddenly he also remembered the principal's question about his name: (10)
"It's English, isn't it?" Being a very black and plain person working in a
minor job, he didn't know what to think about this. And didn't the prin-
cipal also advise him to go to the school library to look up his name in one (11)
of the books? But the kids, what would they think and say when he turn-
ed up there? They would surely stare at him and giggle all the time. And (12)
he knew that his reading abilities were very poor. No, he wouldn't go (13)
there.
The janitor locked the main entrance, went around the building and tried (14)
the side doors as usual. But this time he kept the big lamp above the main
entrance switched on. And in a loud voice he said to himself: "Finished, (15)
Mr. Ralph Mumsford." Then he turned, crossed the playground followed
by the long rays of bright light and proudly walked down the moonlit road (16)
to his home swinging the bunch of school keys with his right hand. (17)

... And now it's your turn

Dennis Kurumada ◆ Just along for the ride (→ pp. 30–32)

Write a continuation of the short story.

Translating texts from English into German

Translation does not mainly mean changing a spoken or written text from one language into another word by word. Special attention has to be given to the author's thoughts and the peculiarities of the foreign language such as style, idioms, etc.

Before translating a text

- Read the translation text and find out its basic meaning.
- Read the text again very slowly paying special attention to details.
- Try to understand what the author wants to say and not only what the words and expressions mean. Get at the deeper meaning behind the words.

While translating a text

- Translate the text sentence by sentence.
- Look up words you do not know in a dictionary.
- Pay special attention to stylistic features, grammatical constructions, tenses, word order, etc. (cf. 'problem areas', p. 80).

- For idioms and collocations find proper German expressions.
- Leave enough space between the lines in your draft for later corrections.
- Do not add alternative solutions in brackets.

After translating a text

- Check your text whether you have really translated everything.
- Go through your translation again and concentrate on the impression the German text gives. If you notice clumsy expressions improve them.
- Write a fair copy.

Problem areas The following examples are syntactic and stylistic peculiarities of English that often cause difficulty when they have to be translated into German.

*** Participle and gerund constructions**	
Examples: **Hearing** the door-bell, he ran to open the door.	**Weil (als)** er die Klingel **hörte**, …
Considering our lack of experience, we did quite well.	In **Anbetracht …**
We'll go for a walk, weather **permitting.**	…, **falls** das Wetter es zulässt.
The **complaints made** about the behaviour of the children …	Die **Klagen über** …
The cars **parked** along the kerb …	Die am Straßenrand **geparkten Autos** …
He succeeded **by working** hard.	**Durch** schweres **Arbeiten** hatte er Erfolg.
On entering the room, he took his hat off.	**Als** er das Zimmer **betrat**, nahm er den Hut ab.
(For further examples see your grammar book.)	

*** Tenses**	
I've been in London for two weeks. If I am late, **I'll take** a taxi.	Ich **bin** seit zwei Wochen in London. … **nehme** ich …
*** Word order**	
Sometimes, **however**, the streets are rather crowded.	Manchmal sind die Straßen **jedoch** sehr belebt.
*** Stylistic features**	
English	**German**
noun The **question** is … It is my personal **belief** …	**verb** Es **fragt** sich, … Ich persönlich **glaube** …
noun At the **top** of his **voice** … They walked back **in silence**.	**adjective** or **verb** … so **laut** er konnte. … **schweigend** …
verb **I'm sure** that he can do this.	**adverb** … **sicherlich** …
passive voice She **was** heartily **thanked** for her help.	**active voice** Man **dankte** ihr herzlich für ihre Hilfe.

Example

English	Comment	German
Police and troops in Northern Ireland are on full alert after a failed bomb attack on a high security prison.	*Troops* = Militär, nicht Truppen. Satzstellung *are / on full alert!*	Polizei und Militär sind in Nordirland nach einem missglückten Bombenanschlag auf ein Sicherheitsgefängnis in höchster Alarmbereitschaft.
It has emerged a vehicle used to transport a bomb and left outside Maghaberry Jail, near Lisburn.	*has emerged* nicht: *kam,* sondern *befand sich.* Present perfect *(has emerged):* Past tense *(befand sich).* Partizipien *used* und *left:* Relativsatz	Die Bombe befand sich in einem Fahrzeug, das zum Bombentransport benutzt wurde und außerhalb des Maghaberry Gefängnisses in der Nähe von Lisburn abgestellt war.
The detonator exploded, but the bomb – weighing nearly 150lb – did not go off.	*but:* jedoch Partizip *weighing:* Relativsatz. Satzstellung!	Die Sprengkapsel explodierte; die Bombe, die nahezu 150 Pfund wog, ging jedoch nicht los.
Dissident republicans opposing the peace process have been blamed for the attack.	Satzstellung! Partizip *opposing:* Relativsatz	Die Schuld an dem Anschlag wird dissidenten Republikanern zugeschrieben, die sich dem Friedensprozess widersetzen.
The explosion occurred at a perimeter gate, usually manned by staff who check identification of the people coming into the jail.	Partizipien *manned* und *coming:* Relativsätze	Die Explosion ereignete sich an einem Außentor, das gewöhnlich mit Personal besetzt ist, das die Identifikation der Leute prüft, die das Gefängnis besuchen.

How to write an exam paper

Writing an **exam paper** is a task to test your knowledge and skills in various ways. The text, the photo, the film clip or the diagram are connected to what you have been dealing with in school. They require you to apply the methods you have practised so far. In *Sekundarstufe I,* exam papers first of all test your knowledge of grammar and vocabulary and your writing skills. In *Sekundarstufe II,* however, the standard of exam papers is higher. They contain different kinds of tasks related to literary and non-literary texts. In school, an interpretation of a literary or non-literary text is usually divided into three or four parts:

1. The reproduction and reorganisation of the content (comprehension/orientation),
2. the close study of formal and structural devices and of language and style (analysis),
3. your personal appreciation of the text as a whole, its meaning and effect (evaluation) and
4. sometimes a translation and explanation of parts of the text and of certain expressions (translation).

Before writing

Reading and pre-writing activities

- Think about your first impression and look at the title, text form/genre, author, date of publication and associations.
- First read the text for gist and get the main idea(s). (→ skimming, p. 12)
- Study the tasks and what they focus on.
- Read the text once more guided by the tasks.
- Check words you need to know to understand the text.
- Underline or mark the parts of the text you are expected to deal with (use different colours for different aspects or tasks).
- Make notes in the margin or on a sheet of paper. Then arrange them in an appropriate order.

While writing

Structuring/composing the text

- Write your answer to each of the tasks on the basis of your notes and refer to what you have marked in the text. Make sure each aspect is covered; tick off what you have tackled.
- Link your answers so that they form a coherent text: Pay attention to the use of
  - a good introduction (→ Topical sentence, pp. 45–46),
  - connectives (→ Connectives, pp. 45, 121),
  - examples and quotations (→ How to quote, pp. 47–49),
  - a conclusion which sums up the gist of the text and the tasks, and, states your personal opinion.

After writing

Checking/ correcting the draft

- Make sure you have covered all the tasks and aspects.
- Check the style of your writing and improve it where necessary.
- Scan your text carefully for language mistakes and correct them.
- Make sure your copy is not only readable but also presentable. When in doubt, write a fair copy.

Example 1: A non-literary text

John Steinbeck ◆ **The making of a New Yorker** (1943)

[…] The transition[1] from small town to New York is a slow and rough process. I am writing it not because I think my experience was unique[2]; quite the contrary. I suspect that the million of New Yorkers who were not born here have had much the same experience – at least parallel experiences … When I came the first time to New York in 1925 I had never been to a city in my life. I arrived on a boat, tourist, one hundred dollars. It was November …

From a porthole[3], then, I saw the city, and it horrified me. There was something monstrous about it – the tall buildings looming to the sky and the lights shining through the falling snow. I crept ashore – frightened and cold and with a touch of panic in my stomach. This Dick Whittington[4] didn't even have a cat.

I wasn't really bad off. I had a sister in New York and she had a good job. She had a husband and he had a good job. My brother-in-law got me a job as a laborer and I found a room three flights up in Fort Greene place in Brooklyn. That is about as alone as you can get. […]

I was going to live in New York but I was going to avoid it. I planted a lawn in the garden, bought huge pots and planted tomatoes, pollinating the blossoms with a water-color brush. But I can see now that a conspiracy was going on, of which I was not even aware. I walked miles through the streets for the exercise, and began to know the butcher and the newsdealer and the liquor man, not as props or as enemies but as people.

I have talked to many people and it seems to be a kind of mystical experience. The preparation is unconscious, the realization happens in a flaming second. It was on Third Avenue. The trains were grinding over my head. The snow was nearly waist high in the gutters and uncollected garbage was scattered in the dirty mess. The wind was cold, and frozen pieces of paper went scraping along the pavement. I stopped to look in a drugstore window where a latexcooch[5] dancer was undulated[6] by a concealed motor – and something burst in my head, a kind of light and a kind of feeling blended into an emotion which if it had spoken would have said, "My God! I belong here. Isn't this wonderful?"

Everything fell into place. I saw every face I passed. I noticed every doorway and the stairways to apartments. I looked across the street at the windows, lace curtains and potted geraniums through sooty glass. It was beautiful – but most important, I was part of it. I was no longer a stranger. I had become a New Yorker. […]

[1] **transition** change – [2] **unique** very special – [3] **porthole** small window on a ship – [4] **Dick Whittington** English folklore: reference to former Lord Mayor of London who had a cat to keep him company – [5] **latexcooch dancer** (Am. sl.) a female exhibition dancer with strong hip movements (compared to waves) – [6] **to undulate** to make movements in the shape of waves

Tasks

Comprehension/orientation

1. Show how the writer manages to give the reader an idea of "the transition" and of the "mystical experience" of being turned into a New Yorker.

   (This task asks you to present the stages from feeling a total stranger to feeling a part of New York City and to point out the secret of that process.)

Analysis

2. Explain how the author employs language to bring his mixed emotions to life.

   (This task asks you to explain how the author frequently refers to his emotions – from shock and fear to happiness – and how he uses the first person singular a lot to stress the subjective quality of his experience; this experience is underlined as something supernatural through the choice of words.)

Evaluation

3. Outline how Steinbeck's presentation of New York's effect on him may help to explain the special attraction of New York, even after the catastrophe of September 11, 2001.

   (This task makes you focus on the very special attraction of NY as an international and multicultural city, a symbol of hospitality to newcomers and of world trade. Even though the city is big and anonymous people help one another. There is something in this city that you cannot explain.)

Solution

John Steinbeck ◆ The making of a New Yorker

Development: from outsider to insider

[…] The transition from small town to New York is a slow and rough process. I am writing it not because I think my experience was unique; quite the contrary. I suspect that the million of New Yorkers who were not born here have had much the same experience – at least parallel experiences … When I came the first time to New York in 1925 I had never been to a city in my life. I arrived on a boat, tourist, one hundred dollars. It was November …
From a porthole, then, I saw the city, and it horrified me. There was something monstrous about it – the tall buildings looming to the sky and the lights shining through the falling snow. I crept ashore – frightened and cold

and with a touch of panic in my stomach. This Dick Whittington didn't even have a cat.

I wasn't really bad off. I had a sister in New York and she had a good job. She had a husband and he had a good job. My brother-in-law got me a job as a laborer and I found a room three flights up in Fort Greene place in Brooklyn. That is about as alone as you can get. [...]

I was going to live in New York but I was going to avoid it. I planted a lawn in the garden, bought huge pots and planted tomatoes, pollinating the blossoms with a water-color brush. But I can see now that a conspiracy was going on, of which I was not even aware. I walked miles through the streets for the exercise, and began to know the butcher and the newsdealer and the liquor man, not as props or as enemies but as people.

I have talked to many people and it seems to be a kind of mystical experience. The preparation is unconscious, the realization happens in a flaming second. It was on Third Avenue. The trains were grinding over my head. The snow was nearly waist-high in the gutters and uncollected garbage was scattered in the dirty mess. The wind was cold, and frozen pieces of paper went scraping along the pavement. I stopped to look in a drugstore window where a latexcooch dancer was undulated by a concealed motor and something burst in my head, a kind of light and a kind of feeling blended into an emotion which if it had spoken would have said, "My God! I belong here. Isn't it wonderful?"

The mystical experience of being a New Yorker

Everything fell into place. I saw every face I passed. I noticed every doorway and the stairways to apartments. I looked across the street at the windows, lace curtains and potted geraniums through sooty glass. It was beautiful – but most important, I was part of it. I was no longer a stranger. I had become a New Yorker. [...]

Task 1: Show how the writer manages to give the reader an idea of the "transition" and of the "mystical experience" of being turned into a New Yorker.

- The information needed to tackle the task has been marked as follows in the text above: development, atmosphere, key words to mark the "mystical experience".
- The information given in the text can be summarised in the following table (the circled numbers refer to the order in which the points will be dealt with in the answer):

first view	direct comment	development	mystical experience
• shocked • frightened • in panic	• slow • rough process • kind of feeling • everything fell into place • mystical experience	• feeling alone • avoiding city • distraction by gardening and other activities	• a flaming moment • becoming a New Yorker • emotional response • different view of everything
①	③	②	④

Answer

Introduction → This is an autobiographical text about the author's experience of landing in New York in 1925 and becoming a part of this city against all his resistance.

Main part ↓

first view — As a young man, the author left a small town in California. When he arrives in New York, he first is shocked and horrified. Although he is supported by relatives who help him to find a job and a place to live, his attitude remains negative. He regards the big city as a "monster".

development — But then he tries to settle down by keeping up his small town habits, e.g. by planting a little garden. And he begins to organise his life. His range of activities becomes wider, he gets to know more people and places and discovers that they are real people.

direct comment — But New York still remains a city which he experiences as rather unfriendly, cold and dirty. The process of becoming a New Yorker is very slow and rough. The writer observes the negative sides of the city very closely. This makes the change in his attitude all the more striking and his "transition" from an outsider to someone who belongs hardly understandable.

mystical experience — In the way he talks about it, it appears almost as a wonder. It is something he cannot explain himself, and obviously it is against all reason. That's why he calls it a "mystical experience".

Conclusion → The problem which Steinbeck is faced with is that he can hardly explain this process of becoming a New Yorker. He can only take notice of the enormous contrast between beginning and end and of the different stages of that transformation.

Task 2: Explain how the author employs language to bring his mixed emotions to life.

- The fact that the writer came from a little town in the West and that this was his first visit to New York has influenced his view of the city; he uses various stylistic means to show this (marked in the text on pp. 84–85), e.g.:

  small town – big city
  darkness – light
  coldness – warmth
  live – avoid living
  world of nature – ugliness of New York
  attraction of the city – unwillingness to live there

  contrast between his real situation and the way he experiences it:
  I wasn't really bad off – negative description of city life
  ugliness of big city – I planted a lawn

- The stylistic devices the author uses to show his personal opinion about life in New York and in a small town can be shown in a list like this:

Use of contrast

- small town world close to nature
- inexplicable attraction of the city
- dirt and ugliness of the city
- unwillingness to be part of it

Use of atmosphere

- darkness and coldness
- ugly city
- light and warmth
- world of nature (gardening)

Use of key words

to refer to what cannot be explained:
I suspect – something monstrous – touch of panic – conspiracy of which I was not even aware – mystical experience – unconscious preparation – realisation in a flaming second – something burst in my head – kind of light, kind of feeling

Use of emotional syntax

- predominant use of "I"
- mostly simple phrases
- accumulation of very short phrases at the end
- exclamations and direct speech: "My God! I belong here."

Answer

←Introduction

The text is not so much about how Steinbeck becomes a New Yorker. It is above all about how he interprets the process of becoming a New Yorker. As a writer, he very consciously uses language to make the reader understand and share his view.

↓ Main part
contrasts

The most striking stylistic device he uses is that of contrast, especially in the form of life in a small town and in a city. He even uses the metaphor of planting to underline the manmade ugliness of the city. But he also uses contrasts to describe what goes on outside and how he experiences it inside. Although he is quite well off (relatives, home, job) he is still critical of the city. His relationship to the city is described in extremes: panic at the monster at the beginning, then his effort to create his own natural world and finally his enthusiasm at belonging. Atmosphere with its contrast of light and darkness and warmth and coldness is another way of describing his changing attitude towards New York.

extremes
atmosphere
key words

His mixed emotion is best expressed in the contradiction of "going to live in New York [...] but going to avoid it" (l. 17). There is something in his relation to New York which he cannot explain; it is something which he can only name "it, something". He describes it as a conspiracy and even as something almost supernatural that happens in a flaming second. This "mystical experience" (ll. 23f.) begins to change his attitude towards people and the city. He is finally forced to give in and accepts joyfully that he is a part of New York. Exclamations like "My God" (ll. 31f.) and extremely plain and short or incomplete sentences indicate the strong emotions. This is also underlined by the personal tone of the text with its predominant use of "I".

emotional use of syntax
"I"

←Conclusion

Although Steinbeck argues that his experience is not unique because it is shared by many immigrants, the text impresses the reader in many ways. First, because it is an important part of the author's life, secondly, because it shows an extraordinary quality of the city that can bring about such an extreme change in one's attitude. A third reason may be that Steinbeck's language reveals what it means to find a home and to feel that you belong.

Task 3: Outline how Steinbeck's presentation of New York's effect on him may help to explain the special attraction of New York, even after the catastrophe of September 11, 2001.

- Gathering ideas, key words and key phrases:

– contrast of small town and this metropolis	(2)
– mystical city which transforms people	(4)
– wonderful sights	(5)
– multicultural atmosphere (melting pot – salad bowl)	(6)
– Sept. 11 disaster	(7)
– symbol of solidarity	(11)
– something very special about New York	(1)
– symbol of living and working together	(10)
– liking and disliking New York	(3)
– city that never sleeps	(8)
– centre of tourism	(9)

- Ordering ideas:

  In the writing task, the ideas can be used as indicated in the list above.

Answer

Introduction → (1) Although Steinbeck says that his experience with New York is not unique, there must be something very special in the relationship between the writer and the city. Otherwise, you cannot explain the transition from extreme panic to enthusiasm in his reaction.

Main part ↓ (2) First there is this enormous contrast between his former home and the giant city which he sees for the first time through a porthole. He is shocked; he is frightened of this monster. The only way of living here is by planting his own natural world. First he does not give New York a chance: He just does not want to live here. There are so many things he does not like in that city that one does not understand why he is beginning to change his
(3) attitude. When he walks through the city he only sees what is ugly. So why does he change? He does not know it himself. He only knows there is something. And the more he thinks and talks about it the more excited he
(4) gets. Until he suddenly realises that this city has a mystical quality which can transform people.

People talking about New York often mention crime and dirt, just like
(5) Steinbeck, but mostly they stress the wonderful sights that are known all
(6) around the world. And the multicultural atmosphere of the city is last but not least reflected in the fact that it is home to the United Nations and was to the World Trade Centre. For a short time all that seemed to have come to an end.

(7) When New York was hit by the terrorist attacks no one believed that the city would come back to life so soon. People all over the world wanted to

help. Perhaps it is only solidarity with the victims and with a city making a new start. But I think it is the same quality which has made New York such a special city: one to welcome strangers from all parts of the world and to offer them a home, and one to win the heart of those, like Steinbeck, who do not like it from the start. And to many, especially young people, it is still the town that never sleeps and offers entertainment around the clock. (8)
No wonder that such a city is like a magnet to tourists who regularly return to the city. They are not afraid. (9)
It is not so much the city itself but what it stands for which makes it so important: a symbol of living and of working together. And after September 11, it is a symbol that terrorism cannot frighten the citizens of New York. (10) They can be sure of the solidarity of the grater part of the world. (11)

← **Conclusion**

... And now it's your turn

E. B. White ◆ Here is New York (1949)

A poem compresses much in a small space and adds music, thus heightening its meaning. The city is like poetry: it compresses all life, all races and breeds, into a small island and adds music and the accompaniment of internal engines. The island of Manhattan is without any doubt the greatest human concentrate on earth, the poem whose magic is comprehensible to millions of permanent residents but whose full meaning will always remain illusive[1]. At the feet of the tallest and plushiest[2] offices lie the crummiest[3] slums. The genteel[4] mysteries housed in the Riverside Church are only a few blocks away from the voodoo[5] charms of Harlem. The merchant princes, riding to Wall Street in their limousines down the East River Drive, pass within a few yards of the gypsy[6] kings; but the princes do not know they are passing kings, and the kings are not up yet anyway – they live a more leisurely life than the princes and get drunk more consistently[7].
New York is nothing like Paris; it is nothing like London; and it is not Spokane[8] multiplied by sixty, or Detroit multiplied by four. It is by all odds[9] the loftiest[10] of cities. It even managed to reach the highest point in the sky at the lowest moment of depression[11]. The Empire State Building shot twelve hundred and fifty feet into the air when it was madness to put out as much as six inches of new growth. (The building has a mooring mast[12] that no dirigible[13] has ever tied to; it employs a man to flush toilets in slack[14] times; it has been hit by an airplane in fog, struck countless times by lightning, and been jumped off by so many people that pedestrians instinctively quicken step when passing Fifth Avenue and 34th Street.)
Manhattan has been compelled to expand skyward because of the absence of any other direction in which to grow. This, more than any other thing, is responsible for its physical majesty. It is to the nation what the white church spire is to the village – the visible symbol of aspiration[15] and faith, the white plume[16] saying that the way is up. The summer traveller swings in over Hell Gate Bridge and from the window of his sleeping car as it glides above the pigeon lofts[17] and back yards of Queens looks southwest to where the morning light first strikes the steel peaks of midtown, and he sees its upward thrust unmistakable[18]: the great walls and towers rising,

the smoke rising, the heat not yet rising, the hopes and ferments[19] of so many awakening millions rising – the vigorous[20] spear[21] that presses heaven hard.
(441 words)

[1] **illusive** illusory (here: *vieldeutig)* – [2] **plushy** luxurious – [3] **crummy** shabby, miserable – [4] **genteel** stylish – [5] **voodoo** African religion – [6] **gypsy** member of the Roma people – [7] **consistent** here: regular – [8] **Spokane** city in Washington State, population about 200.000 – [9] **by all odds** all in all – [10] **lofty** impressively high – [11] **depression** period of weak economy, here: 1929 – [12] **mooring mast** used to fasten a balloon or an airship [13] **dirigible** airship like a Zeppelin – [14] **slack** here: not busy – [15] **aspiration** here: *Ehrgeiz* – [16] **plume** feather – [17] **pigeon lofts** part of a house under the roof where pigeons are kept – [18] **upward thrust unmistakable** upward push which cannot be overlooked – [19] **ferment** here: forms of unrest – [20] **vigorous** strong – [21] **spear** *Speer*

Tasks

1. How does the author define New York in the different paragraphs?
2. Comment on at least three different stylistic devices which try to catch the particular quality of the city. Show what kind of images they evoke.
3. Outline what the text tells you about the author and the kind of reader he may have in mind.
4. Translate the last paragraph trying to catch the spirit of the original. (→ Translating texts from English into German, pp. 79–81)

Example 2: A literary text

Langston Hughes ◆ Early autumn

When Bill was very young, they had been in love. Many nights they had spent walking, talking together. Then something not very important had come between them, and they didn't speak. Impulsively, she had married a man she thought she loved. Bill went away, bitter about women.
Yesterday, walking across Washington Square, she saw him for the first time in ten years.
"Bill Walker," she said.
He stopped. At first he did not recognize her, to him she looked so old.
"Mary! Where did you come from?"
Unconsciously, she lifted her face as though wanting a kiss, but he held out his hand. She took it.
"I live in New York now," she said.
"Oh" – smiling politely. Then a little frown came quickly between his eyes.
"Always wondered what happened to you, Bill."
"I'm a lawyer. Nice firm, way downtown[1]."

"Married yet?"

"Sure, Two kids."

"Oh," she said.

A great many people went past them through the park. People they didn't know. It was late afternoon. Nearly sunset. Cold.

"And your husband?" he asked her.

"We have three children. I work in the bursar's[2] office at Columbia[3]."

"You're looking very …" (he wanted to say *old*) "… well," he said.

She understood. Under the trees in Washington Square, she found herself desperately reaching back into the past. She had been older than he then in Ohio. Now she was not young at all. Bill was still young.

"We live on Central Park West," she said. "Come and see us sometime."

"Sure," he replied. "You and your husband must have dinner with my family some night. Any night. Lucille and I'd love to have you."

The leaves fell slowly from the trees in the Square. Fell without wind. Autumn dusk[4]. She felt a little sick.

"We'd love it," she answered.

"You ought to see my kids." He grinned.

Suddenly the lights came on up the whole length of Fifth Avenue, chains of misty brilliance[5] in the blue air.

"There's my bus," she said.

He held out his hand, "Good-bye."

"When …" she wanted to say, but the bus was ready to pull off[6]. The lights on the avenue blurred[7], twinkled[8], blurred. And she was afraid to open her mouth as she entered the bus. Afraid it would be impossible to utter a word. Suddenly she shrieked very loudly, "Good-bye!" But the bus door had closed.

The bus started. People came between them outside, people crossing the street, people they didn't know. Space and people. She lost sight of Bill. Then she remembered she had forgotten to give him her address – or to ask him for his – or tell him that her youngest boy was named Bill, too.

(441 words)

[1] **downtown** here: business centre of Manhattan – [2] **bursar** person responsible for handling finances – [3] **Columbia** private university situated in New York City – [4] **dusk** time before nightfall – [5] **brilliance** brightness – [6] **to pull off** to start to leave – [7] **to blur** to become unclear – [8] **twinkle** light changing

Tasks

1. Point out what the story is about and what inner development is presented. **Comprehension/ orientation**

   (You are asked to concentrate on the meeting and the contrast between the small talk and the deep effect it has on the woman.)

2. Explain how dialogue, setting and atmosphere are related to one another. **Analysis**

   (You are expected to show how, contrary to the dialogue, the suppressed emotion of the woman is reflected in the rich associations of New York in autumn.)

3. Choose between one of the following two tasks:

Evaluation

3.1 Point out the different devices the author uses to create an intimate, familiar mood and to get the reader emotionally involved.

(Your task is to show how different devices – such as point of view, imagery and symbolism, furthermore the use of contrasts and key words and irregular syntax – work together to stimulate an emotional response of the reader.)

or:

Creative production (personal letter)

3.2 In a letter to her mother in Ohio, Mary writes about the unexpected meeting to show what she feels and how she sees her life after leaving Bill.

(Your letter should focus on the psychological involvement and the review of Mary's past which lays open what is only hinted at in the text.)

Solution

Langston Hughes ◆ Early autumn

love in the past; separation; narrator's comment

When Bill was very young, they had been in love. Many nights they had spent walking, talking together. Then something not very important had come between them, and they didn't speak. Impulsively, she had married a man she thought she loved. Bill went away, bitter about women.

meeting; narrator's comment; different behaviour

Yesterday, walking across Washington Square, she saw him for the first time in ten years.

"Bill Walker," she said.

He stopped. At first he did not recognize her, to him she looked so old.

"Mary! Where did you come from?"

Unconsciously, she lifted her face as though wanting a kiss, but he held out his hand. She took it.

"I live in New York now," she said.

Bill's and Mary's reaction; dialogue: exchange of information

"Oh" – smiling politely. Then a little frown came quickly between his eyes.

"Always wondered what happened to you, Bill."

"I'm a lawyer. Nice firm, way downtown."

"Married yet?"

"Sure. Two kids."

"Oh," she said.

A great many people went past them through the park.

People they didn't know. It was late afternoon. Nearly sunset. Cold.

"And your husband?" he asked her.

narrator's comment; narrator's comment

"We have three children. I work in the bursar's office at Columbia."

"You're looking very ..." (he wanted to say *old*) "... well," he said.

She understood. Under the trees in Washington Square, she found herself desperately reaching back into the past. She had been older than he then in Ohio. Now she was not young at all. Bill was still young.

"We live on Central Park West," she said. "Come and see us sometime."

"Sure," he replied. "You and your husband must have dinner with my family some night. Any night. Lucille and I'd love to have you."

narrator's comment

The leaves fell slowly from the trees in the Square. Fell without wind. Autumn dusk. She felt a little sick.

"We'd love it," she answered.

"You ought to see my kids." He grinned.

Suddenly the lights came on up the whole length of Fifth Avenue, chains of misty brilliance in the blue air.
"There's my bus," she said.
He held out his hand, "Good-bye."
"When …" she wanted to say, but the bus was ready to pull off. The lights on the avenue blurred, twinkled, blurred. And she was afraid to open her mouth as she entered the bus. Afraid it would be impossible to utter a word. Suddenly she shrieked very loudly, "Good-bye!" But the bus door had closed.

bus comes between them
narrator's comment

The bus started. People came between them outside, people crossing the street, people they didn't know. Space and people. She lost sight of Bill. Then she remembered she had forgotten to give him her address – or to ask him for his – or tell him that her youngest boy was named Bill, too.

people come between them
second separation

Task 1: Point out what the story is about and what inner development is presented.

- The evidence your findings should be based on is marked yellow for the plot.
- Violet is for Mary's and Bill's inner development, the theme of the story.
- Atmosphere is marked blue.

Collecting ideas:

Plot	Inner development		
Past	**Mary**		**Bill**
• walking and talking together • love suddenly came to an end • Mary married s.o. else • Bill went away	she thought she was in love	↔	in love first separation bitter about women
Present	**Mary**		**Bill**
• meet again after years • talk about their families • autumn dusk, leaves fall from trees • second separation: bus ready to pull off; couldn't make a date and exchange addresses	• recognizes him, wanting a kiss • three children • invites Bill to see her • felt a little sick • afraid, shrieking 'good-bye'		• holding out his hand, • thinks she looks so old • two kids • invites her for dinner • indifferent, neutral • no reaction

Ordering ideas and planning the text:

What happens on the face of things:

- *Mary and Bill accidentally meet in New York*
- *Exchange of latest news:*
  - Mary (who had left Bill) is married; three children
  - Bill is married: two children
  - Exchange of invitations
- *Traffic situation: arrival and departure of bus*

What the meeting and the separation mean to both of them:

- Bill: neutral and formal
- Mary: emotionally involved, but understands that Bill does not love her any more; desperate and sick

Answer

Introduction
meeting in New York ➜

Two people who were in love when they were young accidentally meet in New York.

Main part ⬇
small talk: exchange of information

The woman, older than the man, had left him years ago to marry someone else. They exchange their latest news: they are both married with three (Mary) and two (Bill) children, have settled in New York, seem to be doing quite well in their work and in their neighbourhood. They finally exchange invitations to meet with their partners.

the real meaning of the meeting

Right from the start, we learn that the meeting means a lot more to Mary than it does to Bill. He remains rather neutral and formal while she is excited and emotionally involved. She first unconsciously wants a kiss to express that former closeness, then gradually begins to understand that their former love means more to her than to him. While the conversation is going on in a neutral and friendly way, we get an insight into the way she feels: desperate and sick, afraid to utter what she wants to say. This may indicate that she still loves him.

Conclusion ➜

In a way, the story is a love story, but not one with a happy ending. It shows that the woman may have made a mistake when she married the other man because her feelings for Bill are still very strong. Bill, however, who felt deeply hurt then, seems to be quite ok. For the woman, it is the second great disappointment.

Task 2: Explain how dialogue, setting and atmosphere are related to one another.

- The paragraphs of the text relevant to deal with this task have been marked blue.
- Notes:
  - *information in the dialogue:*
    where they live, what they do; their families; invitation; small talk, i.e. the usual exchange of information (on the face of things); below the surface information on the former love and on the present disappointment
    ➜ highly formal, conventional, dialogue underlining distance
  - *information on setting (time and place):*
    anonymity of a big city like New York; individual lost in a mass: isolation and loneliness
    ➜ sad mood shown in urban setting
  - *information on atmosphere:*
    autumn; dusk, nearly sunset; cold; early autumn, the leaves falling slowly from the trees indicating something coming to an end; atmosphere of luxury of Central Park and famous shopping streets contrary to emotional loss
    ➜ atmosphere stressing the feeling of something having come to an end

- Planning the text:
  - the previous history: love; the meeting and separation; the question what it is all about — **Introduction**
  - the conventional small talk and what is hidden by it: the different reactions of Mary and Bill: involvement vs. distance — **Main part 1**
  - the function of setting and atmosphere: isolation and loneliness; implication of end — **Main part 2**
  - the real significance of the story — **Conclusion**

Answer

← Introduction

On the face of things, the reader wonders what is worth telling in this story. A man meets a woman he once loved, and before they can arrange to meet they are separated again. What makes this story interesting, however, is what happens inside the woman. That we do not get to know directly, through the dialogue, but more through the description of setting and atmosphere.

↓ Main part dialogue

The dialogue in this story serves as an exchange of information on what one needs to know when meeting after many years. Contrary to Bill's indifferent reaction, the narrator indicates that to Mary the meeting leads to the awareness of being old, of being sadly disappointed and of feeling sick. At the same time she is keeping up a conversational tone. There is, however, something she really wants to say but feels afraid to utter.

setting and atmosphere

What the reader already guesses from the description of how she acts and speaks is underlined by the setting and the atmosphere of the story. The anonymity of a city like New York with its thousands of people passing by emphasises the sense of isolation and loneliness of the individual, here Mary. And the atmosphere of wealth and luxury such as Central Park West and fashionable shopping streets stand in contrast to the emotional loss which Mary feels. Moreover, early autumn with its dusk and coldness and its falling leaves foreshadows some sort of end.

← Conclusion

The meaning of the encounter of the two former lovers becomes clear not so much through what is shown but how it is shown, i.e. that even the good quality of life and the light and fascination of New York cannot brighten your life if you feel lonely. The busy life of all the other people in New York and nature preparing for the winter season stresses Mary's loss and frustration and makes this reunion of former lovers meaningful for a wider audience.

Task 3.1: Point out the different devices the author uses to create an intimate, familiar mood and to get the reader involved emotionally.

- Somehow, the reader sympathises with Mary. Apart from the narrator's direct comments, there are less obvious devices. They are meant to show how important the meeting is for Mary and to stimulate the reader's emotional response (special atmosphere and the use of metaphors, symbols and irregular syntax).
- Collecting ideas:

  (1) feeling of love, disappointment, longing and sad memory; feeling of lost youth — **Topic/theme**

List of predominant devices:

Point of view (2) third-person narrator taking Mary's side; narrator's comments make the reader understand and feel sympathy with Mary

Structure/ contrast (3) reunion in an anonymous town during rush hour; new beginning and the sense of a near end, autumn; trying to remember and reach into the past; forgetting ("she remembered she had forgotten")

Metaphor/ symbol (4.1) early autumn, autumn leaves falling: end

(4.2) separation, too late; people came between them: end of their relationship

Setting (5) New York, huge city making an individual feeling unimportant

Atmosphere (6) autumn, dusk, coldness, late afternoon: sadness

Style (7) in the narrative part short sentences and the use of "I": personal, emotional way of speaking in the dialogue: formal, polite, non-committal

- Arranging the ideas and planning the text in a flow chart:

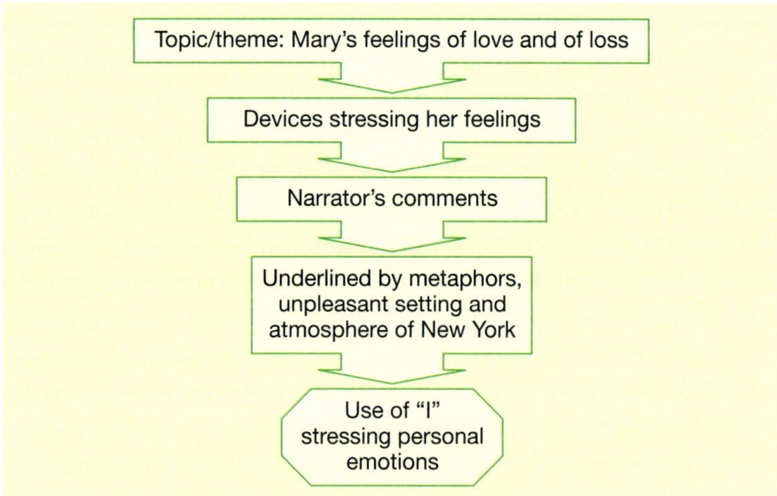

Answer

Introduction→ The story is about first love, separation and reunion, but also about loss and disappointment.

Main part↓ The feeling of lost love is never directly mentioned, it is only indirectly revealed; above all, in the contrast between the superficial exchange of information and small talk. It is used here to hide Mary's feelings (of love and of loss) and Bill's rather formal reaction.

topic

From what happens this story is just about an accidental meeting of two former lovers after ten years. It is through the point of view which is most obvious in the narrator's comments that the reader gets to know about what goes on inside Mary. Mary wants to let her feelings out but can't. She

stylistic devices

suddenly feels old and desperate. What the narrator remarks is underlined by metaphors taken from nature, e.g. falling leaves, a cold and unpleasant atmosphere and the setting of New York. It is the big city in which the individual can feel terribly alone although he or she is surrounded by masses of people. The metaphors and the symbol of nature and the season stand for the sense of time passing by. It is too late for their love. The syntax with the frequent repetition of "I" is used to stress the very personal emotion which is too strong to be controlled.

All in all, the short story presents quite a common situation: old friends meet again. The point of view of the third-person narrator makes the reader look at the meeting through Mary's eyes. So an ordinary moment becomes quite meaningful and stimulates the reader's emotional reaction: that of sympathy and pity. ←**Conclusion**

Task 3.2: In a letter to her mother in Ohio, Mary writes about the unexpected meeting to show what she feels and how she sees her life after leaving Bill.

- The personal letter allows you to write about what Mary thinks and feels from her point of view. A lot might go on inside her head. Notes:

Collecting ideas

- sth. happened yesterday
- met Bill
- Washington Square
- still attractive
- still looks young
- lawyer
- nice autumn afternoon
- first didn't recognise me
- my first love
- I was older than Bill
- thought I loved another man
- mistake to leave Bill
- now married, three kids
- Bill has grown cold
- dream of living in New York
- tired of living in Ohio
- one has dreams
- exchanged invitations
- bus
- no address

Selecting and organising ideas – planning the text

the meeting
- sth. happened yesterday
- met Bill, my first love
- still attractive

the reflection
- was it right to leave Bill?
- difference in age
- meeting him brought it all back
- feeling that I miss sth.
- why did I meet him?
- have to be content with what I have
- but nice to talk to Bill and meet his family

Answer

Dear Mum,

Sorry I haven't written for such a long time. Everything's fine so far, apart from, well, you know, something that happened yesterday and has kept me awake and thinking ever since. You remember Bill, my high school love? Imagine, he's in New York and I just met him on my way home from the office. He hasn't changed much. Still very attractive! He's married and has got two kids. Talking to him has brought it all back. I was so young

then, and Bill was even younger. I thought our love would not have had a chance. I couldn't stand living in our little town any longer. I wanted to go to college, and he was still in high school. And when John asked me to marry him and move to New York, I thought that was the answer to my problem.
And it all seemed right. I love my family, I love my job though I sometimes think there is something missing. You know, mum, I'm not so sure now. I am asking myself if it was a mistake to leave Bill. But now it's too late. There are some things in life you can't correct.
I do wonder what led Bill to cross my way home. Wasn't it to remind me of what I should be grateful for, my family, my job, my life in general? Or was it to tell me that one should still have dreams of what one can do better, to fight against boredom and frustration? Still, I think, it must be nice to talk to Bill and to meet his family. I should be able to find out where he lives with his family – and then we might have a reunion of our two families.

Love,
Mary

... And now it's your turn

Ernest Hemingway ◆ At two o'clock in the morning
(1927, published in 1947)

At two o'clock in the morning two Hungarians[1] got into a cigar store at Fifteenth Street and Grand Avenue. Drevitts and Boyle drove up from the Fifteenth Street police station in a Ford. The Hungarians were backing their wagon[2] out of an alley. Boyle shot one off the seat of the wagon and one out of the wagon box. Drevitts got frightened when he found they were both dead. "Hell, Jimmy," he said, "you oughtn't to have done it. There's liable[4] to be a hell of a lot of trouble."
"They're crooks[5], ain't they" said Boyle. They're wops[6], ain't they? Who the hell is going to make any trouble."
"That's all right maybe this time," said Drevitts, "but how did you know they were wops when you bumped[7] them off?"
"Wops," said Boyle, "I can tell wops a mile off."

[1] **Hungarian** inhabitant of Hungary (*Ungar)* – [2] **wagon** station wagon used for transporting goods – [3] **to be liable to** to have a tendency to – [4] **crook** (infml.) criminal – [5] **ain't they** (infml.) aren't they – [6] **wop** (US acronym) person **w**ithout **o**fficial **p**apers, illegal immigrant – [7] **to bump off** to kill

Tasks

1. Give a factual account of what the story is about.
2. Show how the characters are presented through action and speech.
3. Put the text into a wider context. Explain what more general problems of life in the United States the story draws attention to.

How to present information

Giving an oral presentation

Giving an **oral presentation** is an important skill in school and in real life. A successful presentation is a combination of talking to an audience and showing pre-prepared visual aids on an overhead projector, on a flip chart or by means of a computer and beamer. It also demands a good command of the language and the ability to catch the listeners' attention to get the subject across. In school there are plenty of occasions for presenting individual or group work, e.g. talking about an important author, giving a book review, a synopsis of a drama or novel or speaking about a controversial topic.

Before giving a presentation

Gathering and organising material

- Collect the necessary ideas for your presentation.
- Use note cards with headings and key points. Do not write out your presentation in full.
- Use only one side of the card.
- Arrange your cards in a logical order and number them.
- Carefully plan what visual aids you want to use to make your presentation lively and informative (e.g. transparencies, flip chart sheets, pictures, and charts).
- Arrange and number your visual aids in the same way as your note cards.
- Transfer those numbers to your note cards and write them below their numbers with a small arrow in front of them (e.g. → 6).
- You may also arrange your notes in a mind map. (→ Mind map, p. 43)
- Check your planned presentation for completeness, clarity of ideas and logical structure.
- Read through and learn your material and notes thoroughly to be well prepared.
- Practise your presentation in front of a mirror or friend. You may also record it on audio- or videotape.
- Do not forget to set a clock to find out how much time you will need for your presentation.
- Finally take care to arrange your material properly and make sure that the technical equipment you want to use works correctly.

Using note cards
Note cards are often used for giving talks and oral presentations. They contain only one topic at a time: a heading and key points to be covered. Note cards provide your memory with the necessary cues. Notes should always be written clearly and in large letters. The cards ought to be numbered in the upper-right-hand corner to prevent them from getting shuffled out of order. The note card method requires that you speak freely and that you practise your presentation before you give it.

Note card

Note card number→ /1/

Transparency number→ → 1

Heading→ *Ray Bradbury: Fahrenheit 451*

Key points→
- *author:* * 1920, American, Los Angeles, successful, many short stories, science fiction
- *book:* published 1953, still read in schools, set in the future, totalitarian state, books banned
- *title:* F. 451 = temperature, books catch fire
- *film:* 1966, show transparency of book cover, explain role of fire brigade

While giving a presentation

- While giving a presentation keep in mind that you want "to sell" interesting content, ideas, etc. and to convince your audience.
- Start with an introduction that will catch the listeners' attention.
- Give a short outline of the topic and main points, which should also be presented by means of the overhead projector or written on the chalkboard or flip chart. You may also distribute an attractive handout.
- Always keep eye contact with your audience for feedback purposes.
- Use short and clearly structured sentences.
- Take care not to use too many new or difficult words your listeners might possibly not know.
- If you use special words and phrases, write them on the board and explain them.
- Repeat or rephrase important points to make sure your listeners understand them better.
- Make short pauses now and then to give your listeners the chance to digest your points.
- Vary the tone and speed of your voice to maintain the listeners' attention.

- Use gestures to support an important point, but use them sparingly.
- Do not distract your audience by walking around without purpose.
- When pointing at your visuals do not use your hand or fingers, use a pen instead.

Finishing a presentation

- In your conclusion, summarise the main points of your presentation.
- Finish with a friendly, humorous remark.
- Switch off the technical equipment you will not need any longer.
- Finally you may encourage your audience to ask questions.

Evaluating a presentation

Evaluating a presentation is a useful way of getting or giving feedback that comprises different aspects, e.g. the speaker's clarity of presentation, his/her abilities to communicate effectively and the listeners' reactions. Together with oral feedback from your listeners an evaluation sheet has proved to be very helpful. In addition it also may serve as a kind of checklist for further presentations.

Evaluation sheet

Note down your comment in key words on the empty lines.

1. Do you feel adequately informed on the subject that was presented?

   ____

   ____

   ____

2. Could you follow the presentation without problems?

   ____

   ____

   ____

3. Did you recognise a logical structure in the speaker's subject matter?

   ____

   ____

   ____

4. Did the speaker use examples and repetition to make difficult points easier to understand?

   ____

   ____

5. Did he/she succeed in maintaining your attention during the presentation?

____

____

____

6. Did you feel to be involved in the presentation?

____

____

____

7. Was the language of the presentation adequate?

____

____

____

8. Did the speaker explain difficult or special words and expressions?

____

____

9. Did he/she speak clearly and loud enough?

____

____

10. How did the speaker handle his/her visual aids and the technical equipment?

____

____

11. Were the visual aids meaningful and did they support the speaker's points?

____

____

____

12. Were the visual aids clearly structured and legible?

____

____

____

13. Did the speaker keep eye contact with his/her audience?

____

____

____

14. How would you evaluate his/her body language?

____

____

____

15. What is your general impression of the presentation? Write down your opinion in complete sentences on a separate sheet of paper.

Presenting a book review

A **book review** is a description and an evaluation of a book. Its purpose is to inform other people about books they may be interested in reading. In a final comment the reviewer puts the subject matter of the book in a wider context and also explains what he/she thinks about the book, its theme and message.

Before writing

- Before you start to read the book, pay attention to its title, cover, front page, preface, table of contents, and blurb on the back cover.
- While reading the book, make notes on the points you would like to mention in your review.
- If you write a review of a work of fiction, also make notes on such elements as character, plot and setting and how they relate to the theme of the book.
- After you have read the book, you may jot down your findings in a grid like the one below and then use them as a guideline for your review.

Notes for a book review of a fictional text:

Bibliographical data	Give the author's name, title of the book, year and place of publication, publisher(s), number of pages.
Classification, genre and topic	What type of book is it (fiction or non-fiction)? What genre does it belong to (biography, detective story, science fiction, etc.)? What topic or theme is it about?
Synopsis of the content	Is the book about the past/present/future time? What happens? Give a description of the development of action and its cause-and-effect structure. What are the characters like? What conflict are they involved in?
Ideas/message	What ideas and message does the book contain?
Personal comment	Write your personal comment and impressions: Was it easy/difficult/interesting to read the book? What especially did you like or dislike? Would you recommend the book?

While writing

- Find a suitable opening sentence to attract the reader's attention.
- Apply a lively style throughout your text to keep him/her interested.
- Use your notes as the basis for writing the review.
- If you write a longer text, use one paragraph for each point.
- It is advisable to write a draft first as you will surely have to make revisions and improvements when re-reading your review.

After writing

- Check if your review is interesting and whether it has a good flow.
- Make sure you have covered the essential points of the book.
- Carefully read through your review, looking for clarity and coherence.
- Re-read your text for language mistakes and correct them.

Example

Ray Bradbury ◆ Fahrenheit 451

The following notes serve as the basis for the review:

Bibliographical data	– Ray Bradbury: Fahrenheit 451. Berlin: Cornelsen, 1999. 158 pages
Time	– the future, 24th century
Classification, genre and topic	– novel, science fiction – authoritarian government, books banned and illegal – free thought and intellectual activities forbidden
Synopsis of the content	– unnamed big city, fire station, different houses, Montag's home, countryside – protagonist: Guy Montag, member of the fire brigade – has to burn down houses where books are found – discontented with his job, society and wife – starts stealing books to read them – discovered by his captain (antagonist) who represents the government – Montag forced to burn down his own house – kills captain and flees to the country to meet intellectuals – war destroys city – Montag helps to establish new and free society
Ideas/message	– social criticism – warning against oppressive governments – freedom of thought is high value
Personal comment	– attractive, interesting book, a lot of action – widens awareness of dangers of censorship – easy reading, book to be recommended

Book review

Bibliographical data →

Ray Bradbury: Fahrenheit 451. Berlin: Cornelsen, 1999. 158 pages

Classification of topic and genre →
Time →

Ray Bradbury wrote this book, which is his most popular novel, in the years following World War II. It deals with life in a society where owning books and reading them is forbidden. As its story is set in the 24th century, it is regarded as a work of science fiction.

Synopsis of the content ↓

At the beginning of the novel the reader meets Guy Montag who works as a fireman. His job is not to put out fires but to set fires to burn books and the houses in which they are kept illegally.

In the course of time Montag develops a growing discontent with his occupation and his life in an authoritarian society. He is also unhappy in his relationship with his wife Millie who is completely addicted to tranquillisers and the virtual world on television and on the radio. One day Montag starts to steal books which he was expected to burn and begins to read them secretly. Before long the captain of the fire brigade is informed about it and orders Montag to set fire to his own house. After burning his home and possessions himself he kills his boss and flees.

On his flight he hears reports that war has been declared. Faber, a retired professor, who shares Montag's criticism of the government advises him to leave the city and flee to the country where he will find a camp of intellectual outlaws, such as former writers, clergymen, and academics, who can help him. The leader of the group tells Montag how the men have each memorised literary works so that some day they can again print books, this time from memory. When bombs destroy the city, the men decide at once to begin anew by creating a society where books and the free thought can flourish and where everyone will be free to grow and learn.

← Ideas/ message

Bradbury wants Fahrenheit 451 to be understood as a social criticism. His message is to warn against the dangers of dictatorship and censorship that prescribe what people have to do and what to think. In these societies people cannot develop as free individuals.

← Personal comment

I was fascinated by this exciting book because it offers an interesting plot full of lively action. Bradbury also widens people's awareness of what life would be like without the right of choosing oneself what to read and do. I can fully recommend this interesting novel, which is also easy to read.

… And now it's your turn

Write a review of a book you have read recently or about a novel or drama (e.g. Macbeth) your class may be dealing with soon and follow the structure of the above example.

Tips for presenting the review

- Present your book review to your class to get feedback and to practise your presentation skills. (→ Giving an oral presentation, pp. 99–101)
- Read out a few interesting passages of the book to your classmates.
- Be prepared to answer questions on the book.

How to understand and analyse visual, audio and audio-visual texts

Visual texts

Visual texts comprise any pictorial representation such as photos, drawings, sketches, caricatures, cartoons, etc. **Cartoons** are drawings in a newspaper or magazine that humorously or satirically criticise current events, usually with a comment or caption (short title) underneath it.

Understanding and analysing a cartoon

Before analysing the cartoon

- Does the caption, if there is one, or the newspaper article which the drawing goes with give you a hint of the problem dealt with?

While analysing the cartoon

- What does the cartoon show in the foreground, background and centre?
- What pictorial elements does the cartoonist use and what do they stand for?
- What does the cartoonist criticise or make fun of?

After analysing the cartoon

- Do you think the pictorial presentation in the cartoon achieves its aim?
- Create a caption, if there isn't any, to express the point made by the cartoonist.

Example

Industrial pollution and man's helplessness (cartoon by Thomas Nast)

Solution

- Topic of the cartoon: Pollution
- Structure: The visual elements

place in cartoon	visual element(s)	meaning
background	group of factories	manufacture of goods
background	smoke from factory chimneys	pollution
centre	waste, dark-coloured water	pollution
background	skeleton (death)	consequence of pollution
foreground	desperate workman	ineffective fight against pollution
foreground	plan	reason for pollution

Analysis

The analysis follows the list of questions on p. 106.

Introduction → context, topic

The cartoon appeared in Harper's Weekly, a New York weekly newspaper, in 1881 at the time a plan to divert the East River round Hunter's point (see note at the bottom of the drawing) was under discussion. The topic of the cartoon mentioned in the caption is 'pollution'.

Main part ↓ visual elements

In the background the cartoon has several factories, near a river, that are causing pollution. They pollute air and water by producing thick smoke and by pumping waste water into the river which, in parts, is now a dark colour. Haunting the place, but scarcely visible, a frightening skeleton is floating amidst the dense smoke from the factory chimneys. In the foreground, the cartoon shows a workman, taller than life, with spade and broom and one hand on his face, probably deeply troubled at the sight of the polluted water and air.

pictorial devices

As has been pointed out the cartoonist uses four pictorial devices to underpin his message: factory smoke and dark-coloured water for pollution, a skeleton showing the consequences of pollution and a desperate man representing our inability to stop pollution.

Helplessness and resignation – a single man with broom and spade struggling against industrial pollution – is represented by a well-ordered composition of symbolic elements.

message

The cartoonist's message is that the pollution of water and air, the essential elements of human life, is a threat to mankind. It can hardly be stopped and often leads to self-destruction and death.

Conclusion → evaluation

By using the visual device of a skeleton the cartoonist emphatically points out that industrial pollution is a serious problem. Scientific findings about the danger of pollution support his message, but the assertion that death follows pollution must, of course, be seen as an exaggeration.

Audio texts

The most important types of **audio text (spoken text)** are news, radio plays, and interviews. You can listen for the main idea(s), the gist, and for details.

Understanding and analysing an interview

Before listening

- Read or listen to the title and the introduction that are often given beforehand and anticipate the contents of the text you are going to hear.
- Ask yourself what you already know about the topic and what you would like to learn.

While listening

You should observe two rules which help you understand a spoken text: Don't strain for every word and, especially in school, apply special comprehension and note-taking techniques.

- Don't worry if you don't understand a word. Listen to the stream of speech and make guesses when things are not clear.

You may want to get all the details of a spoken text or only the main idea(s), the gist.

Listening for gist

- Jot down key words in an unorganised manner while listening:

key word(s) key word(s)

key word(s) …

Listening for detail

- Listen for gist first, arrange the key words, listen again and enter details (notes, not complete sentences!) in a note-taking chart while and after listening:

key word(s)	key word(s)	key word(s)	…
(notes)	(notes)	(notes)	
…	…	…	

The note-taking chart for a radio play could look like this:

event	setting	character(s)	…

After listening

- Complete your note-taking chart.
- Think of points you would like to talk about in class.

Example

An interview on American youth

Ask somebody to read the text out to you.

The interviewer and Peggy Pennock talk about some traits in young Americans.

INTERVIEWER: Peggy, as an English teacher at Ferndale High School in Michigan, you are very close to young American students. You speak to them every day both inside and outside the classroom. After the much publicised school killings, how wild and violent are American students really?

PEGGY PENNOCK: Good question. I think American students as a whole are really not wild or violent. That's just a perception of the media, and you know how the media like to exaggerate things to get people stirred up. Incidents of violence in schools have actually been declining in the United States. The kids I know are really concerned about a safe learning environment. School for them is like a second home, and they have just as many fears as anyone else about knowing that a classmate may have a gun or knife on him or in their locker. And the truth of the matter is they don't want anything wild or violent to occur in their schools.

INTERVIEWER: Oh, I see. And I'm sure you're right. But you mentioned you were a guest once on a program about date rape. How prevalent is date rape among American teenagers, and what causes it?

PEGGY PENNOCK: That's a good question, too. Date rape is very prevalent amongst American teenagers. And I think the cause, this is going to surprise you, I think the cause stems from the feminist movement. I know that's shocking, but let me explain. The feminist movement declared women to be equal to men in every sense of the word. And men, unfortunately, are promiscuous beings. And so women thought, aha, if we're equal to men, and now that we have a birth control pill, we can be equally as promiscuous. And men saw women in a different light. No longer were females placed on a pedestal, an object of worship and admiration and respect. Instead, women have become to men an object for sexual pleasure, sexual play. So date rape in America has been something that has occurred a lot, and sadly enough, it's due to some of the influences of the feminist movement.

Before listening

- The title and the introduction to the interview don't give any hints at the points the text will deal with. But you have certainly heard a lot about American teenagers and shootings in American schools.

While listening

First listening: listening for gist

- The interview deals with two aspects: the key words to be jotted down are "violence in schools" and "date rape".

Second listening: listening for detail

- Peggy Pennock
  on violence in schools
  - students not violent or wild
  - students concerned about safety in schools
  - they don't want anything violent in their schools

  on date rape
  - very prevalent among teenagers
  - due to feminist movement
  - women: objects for sexual pleasure

After listening

The situation in America and Europe (Germany) could be compared.

Audio-visual texts

TV-news, documentaries, feature films, etc. are all **audio-visual texts**. A feature film is the most popular audio-visual text. It is an important source of information on the context of the English-speaking world; and it is a modern art form that education cannot neglect, especially when it comes to literature turned into film. Dealing with the language and message of films is an important part of media literacy.
A lot of what has been said about working with texts applies to film, too. But in a way, a film is more complex than a text because it makes use of other codes (image and sound) in addition to the text. A film speaks, first of all, through images which in the process of their being shot, cut and edited are influenced by many people and procedures. The work of the actors and film architects is directly visible. The work of the director or the cameraman (or woman) is ultimately responsible for what we see.
When dealing with a film in class you will get to watch the relevant parts of a film more than once, at least twice. So you can concentrate on various elements of the film. The different columns of the viewing grid on p. 112 will help you to fill in the results of the different watching processes.

Understanding, analysing and evaluating a (video)film

Before watching

Expectations/ associations/ predictions

Study the presentation of a film on a poster or on the cover of the video or DVD to get an idea of what the film may be about, e.g.:

- Start with the (original) title of the film. What does it make you think of?
- Analyse the poster or the different still photographs to imagine the kind of action or the problem presented.

- What kind of film do you connect with the names of the director and of the leading actors?
- Have you ever heard of the book the film or the script is based on?
- What do you know about how the film was received by the public or by the critics?
- How is the film advertised, i.e. how is it described to attract viewers?
- What do you know about the year when it was released?
- What does the rating of the film indicate?
- What film category or genre does the film belong to?

While watching

First presentation

You should first concentrate on **what** is shown (surface structure – content analysis). This usually means:

What is presented?

- What kind of **action** can be observed? What happens in the outside world, what goes on inside a character? Can you observe a development? What are the distinctive stages?
- What **characters** can you make out? Are there visible distinctions such as gender, age, social class? What does their presentation tell you about who they are, what they do, what role they play and what problem they may be faced with?
- What is the **place of action/setting**? Where does the action take place? What different spots can you distinguish? How are they linked with the character(s)? How are they connected with the kind of action you can observe? Does the place have a special atmosphere? How do **setting** and **atmosphere** go together?
- Fill your findings and observations into the columns of a viewing grid:

action	characters	place and time of action/ setting	field sizes, camera angles, etc.	sound-track	further observations/ impressions

Second presentation

You should now concentrate on **how** action, character(s) and setting are presented with the help of the language of film (deep structure – formal analysis). For information and orientation see the **film lexicon** and the **still** on p. 113.

How is it presented?

- How much are you allowed to see? Do you get the complete picture or only a fragment of it? Why do you think the particular **field size** was used? What effect would a different field size have on the viewer?
- From where do you get to see what you see? Why was the special position of the camera, the **camera angle**, chosen to shoot that scene? What would it mean for the observer/viewer if the opposite camera angle had been used?
- What does it mean that the camera (or the lens) is not in a fixed position but able to move from right to left, up and down, in and out? What is the advantage of these **camera movements** as opposed to a camera in a fixed position?
- In general, the camera is the viewer's eye. Still, ask why you are made to watch a certain scene through the eyes of a certain character, why you are made to watch the scene from his or her **point of view (POV)**?
- The **soundtrack** of a film is often composed or arranged to heighten the tension or to deepen a certain effect and create a specific mood. Background noises are mixed with music (vocal or instrumental). It has sometimes been specifically composed to go with the film. In general, you find a connection between the lyrics of a song and the message of the scene. Among one of the most effective ways to use the soundtrack is **silence**.

The film lexicon

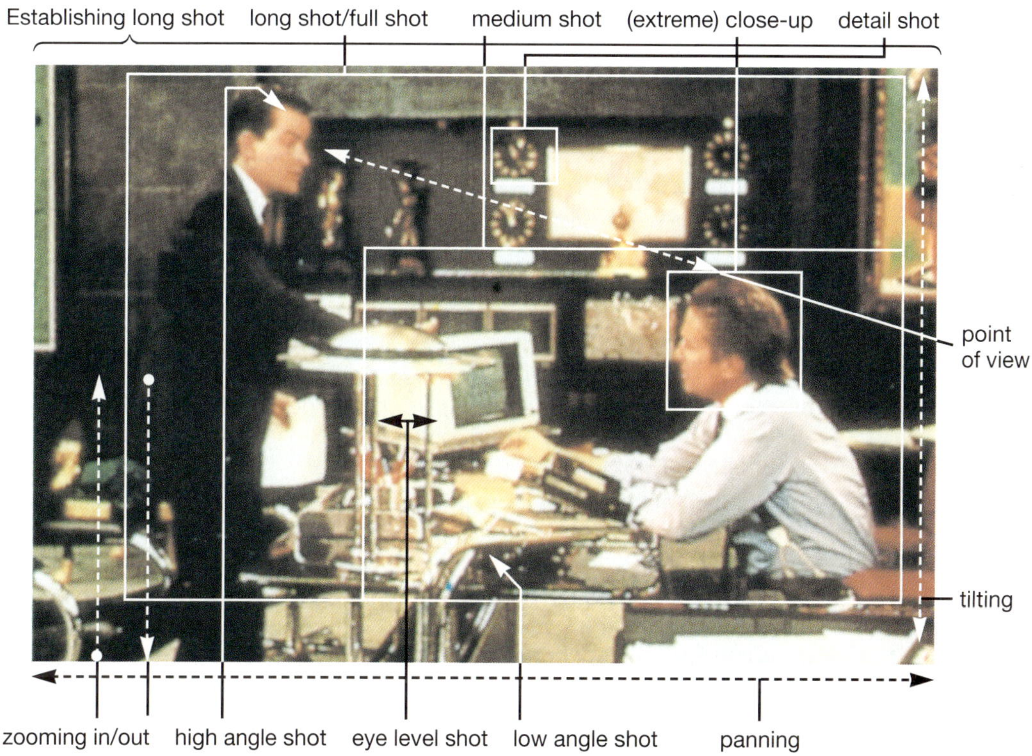

Film language: How it works and what effect it has

Soundtrack • music: famous songs or especially composed film music • all kinds of background noises • silence	used to show the authenticity of the place, to underline the atmosphere and mood of the scene and to create tension
Field sizes • (establishing) long shot • full shot, medium shot • (extreme) close-up, detail shot	the different sizes of the pictures you see are used to give you an overall picture, keep you at a certain distance or make you feel close to the action
Camera angles • high angle (overhead/bird's eye) • eye-level (straight-on angle) • low angle (below shot)	camera positions are chosen to make the person or object seem less prominent, more or less normal or rather impressive
Camera movement • panning (from side to side) • tilting (up and down) • zooming in/out • tracking shot	allowing the viewer's eyes to adapt to the gradual unfolding of the picture and to make him aware of the transition from one picture to the next or following a character's steps to stress his advancement
Point of view (POV) • shot from the position of one of the characters • over-the shoulder-shot • reverse-angle-shot	• presenting a scene as viewed by a character • underlining the role of a speaker or listener in a dialogue • emphasising the opposite side

After watching

Third presentation

Finally, concentrate on the interaction/interdependence of all the various factors. What is their overall meaning (deep structure – evaluation of meaning)?

What does it mean?

- Complete your viewing grid (after the third presentation). What further details have you been able to observe? Where in the grid do they belong?
- How can the observations be classified or ranked according to importance (1., 2., …)? Where does your very personal response come in? Why may that be important to you? Think of the role of e.g. the music or silence!
- How do the results of the content analysis relate to the observations of the formal analysis (e.g. emphasis, contrast, illustration, modification, variety, provocation, etc.)?
- Now interpret the function of the formal element with regard to the content. Why has the particular field size or camera angle been chosen to show the action or present the character? What do other ways of shooting the scenes add to what you already know about the action and the character(s)? What is the total effect of the variety of film language in the different cuts?

- Have your expectations with regard to title, advertising and public response been fulfilled? If not, how do you judge your own reaction? Can you give reasons why you are disappointed?

Example

Oliver Stone (Director) ◆ Wall street

The twelve stills give you an impression of

1. the theme of the film and the character and action it is based on,
2. the work of the camera man trying to catch the atmosphere of the place and
3. to demonstrate how the soundtrack supports the presentation of visual message.

The stills represent above all the variety of film language. They, however, do not fully illustrate how the pictures and the mini scenes are **cut**, i.e. put together in a kind of montage to create the special meaning (e.g. of the world of high finance where the sky is the limit; compare Sinatra's song "Fly me to the moon ..."). The film is available on video and DVD.

1

- establishing long shot
- Sinatra: "Fly me to the moon, let me sing among those stars. Let me see what spring is like on Jupiter and Mars."

2

- panning
- traffic noises overlapping Sinatra, "In other words, hold my hand"

3

- close-up
- noise of train in motion overlapping Sinatra, "You are all I long for"

4

- panning in fast motion, blurred images
- Sinatra, "In other words, I love you."

5

- medium shot, high angle shot
- song (instrumental), traffic noises

6

- below angle shot
- song (instrumental), traffic noises

7

- zooming in
- Sinatra "Fill my heart with song"

8

- high angle shot, close-up
- voices overlapping Sinatra, "I love you"

9

- from long shot to tracking shot
- office chat, "How you're doin', buddy?" – "Great …"

10

- long shot
- voice over: "Think of the fundamentals. That's how IBM and Hilton were built. Good things sometimes take time."

11

- zooming in
- office noises, chatter

12

- extreme close-up, detail shot
- voice over: "OK. Let's go to work!"
- ringing of a bell

Solution

The viewing-grid

action	characters	place of action/ setting	field sizes, camera angles, etc.	soundtrack/ music
commuters on their way to work by car, underground, on foot, on escalators, in elevators, passing all the sights of the city; distinctive young man fighting his way through the masses; constantly reading, ignoring his environment until he has reached the top	one young man on his way to his Wall Street office in Downtown Manhattan; his fellow commuters; the masses in his way; his colleagues in the office; no one really taking notice of him	New York skyline (with the World Trade Center) at dawn, harbour scene, in the underground, on the escalator, in the streets of Downtown Manhattan, in the lobby of office building, in the elevator, in the office	establishing long shot, tilting, panning, close-up, extreme close-up, bird's eye view (high angle), below shot (low angle), normal shot (eye-level), tracking shot	no dialogue at the beginning, Frank Sinatra love song ("Fly me to the moon") interrupted by background noises (traffic noises overlapping the song), office chat and business talk (about great success stories: IBM, Hilton) and talk on the phone

The overall meaning

The ideas which the audience links with Wall Street are confirmed in the trailer. It not only introduces the cast but presents the theme of the film: a man on his way through the jungle of the business district of Manhattan and on his way up. All the images and the handling of the camera and cutting technique stress how unimportant the individual is which is shown here as a little piece functioning in traffic and commuting, being dragged and driven by the masses surrounding him. When he arrives in his office the ideas and images of big business take over. The viewers may expect a film on some variation of the American Dream, the urban success story. They may also expect a story of a young man whose dreams of striking it rich will be shattered. It can also be the story of a young ambitious man who will either make his way or will be corrupted.

Vocabulary for text analysis and text production

Author

the author	wants to	influence	the reader	
		persuade		(*überreden*)
		convince		(*überzeugen*)
		impress		
		inform		
		entertain		(*unterhalten*)
	is concerned with …			(*befassen*)
	deals with …			
	speaks about …			
	discusses …			
	gives his opinion		on the problem of …	
			on the question of …	
	expresses his point of view concerning			(*Meinung*)
	holds the view that …			
	comments on …			
	gives an exact analysis of …			
	gives a personal interpretation of …			
	presents the thesis that …			
	puts forward	an argument	against …	
		arguments	for …	
	provides	evidence	in support of …	(*Beweis*)
	gives			
	assumes that …			(*annehmen*)
	supposes that …			
	refers to an example			(*sich beziehen auf*)
	draws the conclusion that …			(*Schluss*)
	comes to the conclusion that …			
the author's	train of thought	is (not) convincing		(*Gedankengang*)
	line of argument			
	opinion is	based on …		
		(not) acceptable		(*annehmbar*)
		(not) questionable		(*anfechtbar*)

Theme

the text	deals with	…	(*handeln von*)
	is about		
	concerns		(*betreffen*)
	presents		
	treats of		(*behandeln*)
	describes		

the theme	of the text	is/are …
topic(s)	of the passage	
main point(s)	of the story	

the general	idea	expressed in the text		is/are …
essential		of the	text	
main			paragraph	

Action

the story takes place in …	(*stattfinden*)
the plot of the story is laid in …	
the scene/action is set in …	
the course of the action	(*Handlungsverlauf*)
the phases / stages of the action	(*Abschnitt*)
the (constituent) elements of the plot	(*konstitutive Elemente*)

Structure

the text	can be divided into	…	parts
story	is divided into		paragraphs
	falls into		chapters
	is composed of		sections
	contains		
	consists of		

the paragraph can be subdivided
the subdivision indicates the sequence of ideas
the constituent elements of the … are …

the first	part	constitutes	the introduction	(*bilden*)
…	paragraph	gives us	central problem	
last	chapter	comprises	principal part	(*umfassen*)
	sentence		solution	

in the	first	part	the author	varies the theme	(*variieren*)
	…	chapter		changes the topic	
	last			goes into detail	
				passes from … to …	

the tension	arises from …
	emerges in …

the scene	is the climax of the	story
dialogue		play
passage		

the climax/turning-point	is reached when …
	comes

the story/play has an open ending

Atmosphere

the atmosphere of the	text is	melancholy	(*melancholisch*)
	passage	gloomy	(*schwermütig, traurig*)
	story		
	play	shown in/by …	

Style

the author	uses	literary	words
	employs	formal	expressions
	makes use of	informal	language
		colloquial	
		familiar	
		slang	

this	word	refers to	…
	expression	underlines	
	phrase	emphasises	
		means	
		stands for	

Characterisation

the author	describes the	characteristics	of …
		outer appearance	
		intellectual qualities	
		mood	
		activities	
		social and psychological condition	
	points out the characteristics of …		
	gives a characterisation of …		
	characterises … (a person as …)		
	gives a	realistic	description of …
		detailed	
	only gives a rough description of …		

the character is	described presented characterised	as …

the basic traits of A's character are …
one of A's striking characteristics is …
A stands in clear contrast to B

Character trait	(*Charakterzug*)		
self-controlled	(*beherrscht*)	easily excited	(*launisch*)
balanced	(*ausgeglichen*)	irritable	(*reizbar*)
calm	(*ruhig*)	impulsive	
patient	(*geduldig*)	intemperate	(*unbeherrscht*)
moderate	(*gemäßigt*)	impatient	
tolerant		bad-tempered	
friendly		intolerant	
good-natured			
benevolent	(*wohlwollend*)		
sensitive	(*sensibel*)	cruel	
modest	(*bescheiden*)	brutal	
self-centred	(*ich-bezogen*)	obstinate	(*eigensinnig*)
aggressive		stubborn	(*halsstarrig*)
ruthless	(*rücksichtslos*)		

Connectives

Adding ideas:
and, also, indeed, as well as, in addition (to), also, further, furthermore, moreover, similarly, in the same manner/way, apart from, equally, little by little, besides, and then, what is more

Enumerating order:
to begin with, next, first(ly), in the first place, secondly, on second thought, above all, on top of (that), then, finally, in conclusion

Exemplifying ideas:
for example, for instance, e.g., such as, thus, to show what (I mean), let us take (the case of)

Expressing place:
here, there, where, in front of, on the right (left), to the right (left), nearby, among, between, in the distance, straight ahead, beside, on the spot

Expressing time:
at first, at last, then, after, before, while, now, since, as long as, as soon as, no sooner than, subsequently, afterwards, in a moment, at the moment, often, initially, previously, recently, momentarily, at the same time, meanwhile, lately, finally, in the end, afterwards, the next (day), eventually, day in – day out, from now on, for the first time, more than once, time and again, many a time

Comparing things:
compared with, in comparison with, likewise, similarly, equally, whereas the former … the latter, in the same way, while the first … the second, as … as, as well

Referring to something:
with reference to, referring to, with regard to, as to, as for, the latter, the former

Contrasting or limiting a statement:
however, but, besides, otherwise, of course, on the other hand, on the contrary, in contrast, despite, still, whereas, maybe, perhaps, nevertheless, instead, yet, apart from, except for, in spite of the fact, nonetheless

Reformulating something:
in other words, that means, that is to say, another way of expressing it, a better way of putting it is, it would/might be better to say, to put it (more) simply, to put it differently

Indicating a consequence or conclusion:
consequently, thus, as a result, for that reason, accordingly, it follows that, then, therefore

Expressing reason and purpose:
for this (that) reason, therefore, that is why, because, because of, so, consequently, since, as, on account of, so that

Inferring from something:
this/that implies, in other words, in that case, otherwise, frankly speaking, then

Expressing condition:
if, unless, provided that, suppose that, on the condition that, in case that

Expressing concession:
though, although, even if, even though, besides, anyhow, anyway, in any case, at any rate, considering

Summing up ideas:
in conclusion, to conclude, all in all, as a result, in brief, on the whole, to sum up, in short

Connecting paragraphs:
Quite a number of the above connectives can also be used to link paragraphs. Some others are:
another point that should be mentioned is, it must also be said that, maybe not everybody knows that, and we must not forget, I would like to add another idea, another argument is

Acknowledgements

Texts

pp. 12–13: "Fox-hunting" from *Encyclopaedia Britannica*, Deluxe 2002 Edition, CD-ROM; **p. 18:** Anthony Storr: "What is agression?" from *Human Aggression* by Anthony Storr, London, Penguin, 1968, p. 32; **pp. 19–20, Solutions p. 1:** Anthony Storr: "Violence in early childhood" from *Human Aggression* by Anthony Storr, London, Penguin, 1968, p. 70; **p. 21:** "Another attack on the river" by Klaus Hinz, first edition; **pp. 22–23, Solutions p. 2:** "Troops on full alert as bomb left outside prison" from *Ananova,* Leeds, April 29, 2002, in: http://www.ananova.com/; **pp. 24–25:** Christopher Cortis, Desmond Clayton: "Foxhunting – for and against" from *Talking of Britain – Einübung in das moderne Englisch* by Clayton, Cortis, Weise, Frankfurt am Main, Fischer, 1970, p. 72; **pp. 26–27, Solutions p. 3:** George Orwell: "Serious sport is shooting minus the shooting" from *Shooting an elephant and other essays* by George Orwell, San Diego, Harcourt Trade Publishers, 1950; **pp. 30–32:** Dennis Kurumada: "Just along for the ride", Reprinted by permision of Scholastic Inc. (Scholastic Writing Award Program). Copyright © 1970 by Scholastic Inc., New York; **pp. 34–35:** Wakaho Yamauchi: "And the soul shall dance" from *Multicultural Scenes for Young Actors* ed. by Craig Slaight, Jack Sharrar, Lyme, Smith and Kraus, 1995, pp. 139–141; **p. 37:** William Soutar: "The children" from *Poems of our time,* ed. by R. Church, M. Bozman, E. Sitwell, London, Everyman's Library 1945; **p. 39:** Wilfred Owen: "Futility" from *The Faber Book of Modern Verse,* ed. by Michael Roberts, London, Faber and Faber, p. 179; **pp. 51–52:** Joseph Bruchac: "The ship" from *New Letters,* 39, No. 2, 1972/73. Reprinted by permission of *New Letters*, University of Missouri, USA; **p. 57:** "Violence and vandalism in American schools" from *Violence and Vandalism. Education U.S.A.*, Copyright © 1977 National School Public Relations Association, Rockville, USA; **pp. 58–59:** "Animals in captivity" by Herbert Holtwisch, first edition; **p. 71:** Sarah Boseley: "Doctors call for total ban on smoking in public" from *The Guardian*, November 7, 2002; **pp. 74–75:** Larry French: "Mr. Mumsford" from *Flash Fiction: Very Short Stories*, ed. by James Thomas, Denise Thomas and Tom Hazuka, New York, W.W. Norton & Co., 1992; **pp. 83–84, pp. 84–85:** John Steinbeck: "The making of a New Yorker" from *New York Observed. Artists and Writers Look at the City,* ed. by Barbara Cohen, Seymour Chwast, Steven Haller, New York, Henry N. Abrams, 1987, p. 122; **pp. 89–90:** E. B. White: "Here is New York" from *New York Observed. Artists and Writers Look at the City,* ed. by Barbara Cohen, Seymour Chwast, Steven Heller, New York, Henry N. Abrams, 1987, p. 121; **pp. 90–91, pp. 92–93:** Langston Hughes: "Early autumn" from *Something in Common and Other Stories.* Reprinted by permission of Farrar, Strauss and Giroux, Inc. Copyright © 1963 by Langston Hughes; **p. 98:** Ernest Hemingway: "At two o'clock in the morning" from *The Essential Hemingway,* Harmondsworth, Penguin, 1964 (repr. 1974), p. 318

Illustrations

p. 30: Volker Kipp; **p. 107:** taken from: Harper's Weekly. Journal of Civilization, August 20, 1881; **pp. 113, 115–116:** Copyright © 1987 Twentieth Century Fox Film Corporation

Register